W9-BKC-807

STUDIES IN COMPARATIVE ECONOMICS 2

Studies in Comparative Economics

1. E. H. Phelps Brown, THE ECONOMICS OF LABOR
2. Charles P. Kindleberger, FOREIGN TRADE AND THE NATIONAL ECONOMY

FOREIGN TRADE AND THE NATIONAL ECONOMY

by Charles P. Kindleberger

NEW HAVEN AND LONDON
YALE UNIVERSITY PRESS

Fourth printing, October 1966.
Designed by Sally Hargrove.
Set in Baskerville type and
printed in the United States of America by
The Carl Purington Rollins Printing-Office
of the Yale University Press.

Library of Congress catalog card number: 62–16236

FOREWORD

Modern economics has been bred chiefly in Western Europe and the United States, and despite its aspiration toward generality it bears the stamp of institutions and issues characteristic of these areas.

But the economic world no longer revolves about London and New York. Dozens of new nations are struggling toward economic independence and industrial growth, under institutional arrangements quite unlike those of the West. Economies of a novel type also extend eastward from central Europe to the Bering Strait and have been busily developing their own principles as a by-product of administrative experience. It is asserted that "Western economics" has only limited analytical value in these other countries.

The problem of the content and relevance of economics thus arises inescapably. Are the economic principles taught in the West really susceptible of general application? Or are they culture-bound and relevant mainly to industrial capitalist countries? Is it possible to create a general economics which would be as useful in Poland or India as in Canada or France? Or must we be content with several species of economics which will remain distinct in intellectual content and applicability?

"Comparative economics" has been regarded as a separate area of the economics curriculum, consisting of a botanical classification of national economies into a few loosely labeled boxes. But surely any course in economics is potentially comparative. A concern with comparative experience can profitably be infused into any of the standard branches of economic study. This series is inspired by the hope that a rethinking of particular branches of economics in world perspective, combined with a bibliography of available material from many countries, may help teachers to give their courses a broader and more comparative orientation.

In pursuing this objective, we deliberately chose autonomy over standardization. Each author was left free to determine his own approach and method of treatment. The essays thus differ considerably in length, analytical as against descriptive emphasis, geographical coverage, and other respects. How far the original intent of the series has been accomplished is for the profession to judge.

We are grateful to the authors who have struggled with possibly insoluble problems, to the Ford Foundation for its support of the enterprise, and to the staff of the Yale University Press for their helpful cooperation.

The Inter-University Committee on Comparative Economics: Abram Bergson, Arthur R. Burns, Kermit Gordon, Richard Musgrave, William Nicholls, Lloyd Reynolds (Chairman)

ACKNOWLEDGMENTS

This short monograph was written during the summers of 1960 and 1961, between intervals of research into problems of French and British economic growth. The imprint of these latter efforts has inevitably rubbed off on it without, it is hoped, causing undue distortion.

My greatest debt is to Charles A. Cooper, who prepared many of the tables and did spadework for the chapter on Soviet bloc trade, in which my comparative disadvantage is greatest. Harry G. Johnson, who served the Comparative Economics Project as a critic, gave me the benefit of his detailed and searching comments above and beyond the call of duty. Franklyn D. Holzman was kind enough to review Chapter 10 and to give me permission to refer to his unpublished work. Robert Barlow, the E.C.E. Steel Division, and the Department of Commerce National Income Unit are among the many people and organizations who responded to requests for specific information. Felicity Hall Skidmore rallied round to nail down a number of references, which poor memory and distance from my home library kept elusive. As on previous occasions Beatrice A. Rogers at M.I.T. edited and typed the manuscript in her efficient, cheerful, and indispensable fashion.

CHARLES P. KINDLEBERGER

Massachusetts Institute of Technology
October 1961

CONTENTS

TABLES

FIGURES

FOREIGN TRADE AND THE NATIONAL ECONOMY

1 INTRODUCTION

The purpose of the monographs in this series is to study a single economic function across a variety of economies, rather than to apply the more traditional, and perhaps less rewarding, method of comparing differently organized economies in all their functional aspects. This purpose is neatly suited to the other monographs in the series. The generality behind capital formation or public finance or agriculture—and the range of differences among economic systems—becomes clear when the single function is studied from country to country. But the analysis of foreign trade, which forms the subject of the present study, has always been comparative. Its foremost principle is embodied in a generalization called "the law of comparative costs," signifying that what a country exports and imports is determined not by its character in isolation but only in relation to those of its trading partners.

If the comparative method in the analysis of foreign trade is not revolutionary, it is true, nevertheless, that there is no brief comparative study of the place of foreign trade in various countries. The present monograph sets out to fill this gap.

It is obviously necessary to limit the subject. We cannot deal in detail with such factors as the determinants of exports and imports, the adjustment mechanism in the balance of payments, international capital movements, or monetary problems. Limitations of space and interest require us to restrict the discussion to two questions:

1. What determines the nature and amounts of the goods a country buys and sells in international trade?
2. What is the impact of foreign trade on national economic life?

We are concerned only with merchandise trade, but in dealing with it we go beyond statics into growth. We want to know how trade changes in the course of economic growth of different countries, and how such growth and other aspects of economic life react under the impact of foreign trade, again under the varying circumstances presented by different countries with their near-infinite variety of resources and of economic and political institutions.

The task presents the usual methodological dilemma: whether to outline a series of case studies and derive principles from them, or to establish a set of principles and garnish them with factual illustration. With the case method it is unclear to what extent the particular circumstances of particular cases may overwhelm the uniformities that may exist beneath the surface; and in any event the wide disparity among cases makes the choice of a small group of "typical countries" next to impossible. On the other hand, the deductive approach runs the risk that material not included may have been discarded because it did not fit a theoretical design. The methodological problem is insoluble, and a choice must be made on the basis of the writer's tastes. We choose to present an analytical framework of the factors that determine how much of what kind of goods a country trades, how this trade changes over time, and what this trade and its evolution do, if anything, for the economic life of the country concerned. We attempt to illustrate the deductive points with empirical material. In the course of the analysis there will inevitably be illustrations that go beyond the narrow point at hand, so that case studies will not be altogether absent: in discussing trade based on natural resources, one must furnish material on the foreign trade of Canada; on labor-intensive exports, the trade of Japan; and so on.

The analysis is qualitative, not quantitative. Economics is only now making the vital transition from qualitative to quantitative techniques; at this stage few econometricians are ready to measure the weight of the various factors that determine a country's exports and imports, and few economists are ready to accept as definitive the measurements set forth by their more daring colleagues. The writer, moreover, is limited by capacity to a literary approach to the problem, supported by only a modest amount of arithmetic. He is thus unable to indicate the relative importance of various factors shaping a country's foreign trade at a particular time, except perhaps in the most general and impressionistic terms. This is admittedly not wholly satisfactory, but it is the best that he can do.

What are the factors determining a country's foreign

trade? Various short statements on the subject can be collected from various authors. We present two, from Kuznets and from Lewis:

> Foreign-trade flows and other movements across national boundaries are affected by many complex factors in which technological changes, social inventions, economic advantages, political revolutions and diversities in the structure and endowments of nations all play their part.[1]

> The extent to which a country participates in international trade depends partly upon its resources, partly upon the barriers it places in the way of trade, and partly upon its stage of development.[2]

As soon as one thinks about the items in any such list, one realizes that they must be dealt with separately to be useful.

The problem in answering our first question is to include all relevant factors. The problem in answering the second is to eliminate all considerations bearing on national economic life other than foreign trade. This too is a tall order. But if we wish to determine the impact of international trade on national life, we must hold all other things equal or, in dealing with historical situations, make allowance for the effect of nontrade influences.

The first and major part of this study, addressed to the question of what determines a country's exports and imports, consists of eleven chapters. Chapter 2 introduces transport costs, which account for the fact that countries do not trade virtually everything. Thereafter we examine the relevance

1. Simon Kuznets, *Six Lectures on Economic Growth* (Glencoe, Ill., Free Press, 1959), p. 106.

2. W. Arthur Lewis, *The Theory of Economic Growth* (London, Allen and Unwin, 1955), p. 340.

of the Heckscher-Ohlin theorem, which explains comparative advantage in terms of factor endowments; in successive chapters, we take up the separate factors of production: natural resources (Chapter 3), labor (Chapter 4), and capital (Chapter 5). Chapter 6 discusses the significance of technology and technological change for foreign trade; Chapter 7, the relevance of a country's capacity to reallocate resources from one occupation to another. A brief Chapter 8 touches upon a neglected topic, the effect on trade of such random factors as war, pestilence, plant disease, and strikes. Chapter 9 deals with monopoly and state interference in predominantly private-enterprise systems. Chapter 10 addresses the complex and little-known subject of foreign trade under socialism. In Chapter 11 we broach the third of Professor Lewis' factors, the vast and widely discussed subject of the impact of economic growth on foreign trade, paying special attention to what we call the "law of declining foreign trade."

The second section, on the effect of foreign trade on the national economy, consists of three chapters. The first, Chapter 12, inverts the subject matter of Chapter 11 and deals with the effect of foreign trade on economic development. Chapter 13 tackles the impact of foreign trade on domestic stability. The final chapter, 14, goes beyond economics narrowly conceived to discuss the relation of foreign trade to the social and political life of nations. Here, among other subjects, we touch on the importance of economics to international political integration.

A selected bibliography on international trade and on the foreign trade of particular countries follows Chapter 14.

2 TRANSPORT AND COMMUNICATION

THE EXISTENCE OF TRANSPORT COSTS

If transport costs for goods[1] were infinite—and if consumers did not commute internationally—there could be no international trade at all. All production would have to be consumed locally. If, on the other hand, transport costs were zero, practically everything would be exchanged in international trade—at least, all goods whose comparative costs of production differed from one place to another. We have yet to discuss comparative costs, but at this stage it is

1. For simplicity of thought and ease of exposition, the discussion is limited to goods, rather than covering both goods and services. Much of what is said about goods applies equally to services, at least as far as comparative costs are concerned. But transport costs of many services border on the infinite. Haircuts are bought nationally, except perhaps by airplane pilots and border workers. Even though services include tourist services, where the consumer is transported to the place of consumption, the proportion of services traded internationally is significantly lower than the proportion of goods so traded. In the United States in

safe to assume that comparative costs would not be identical for many commodities.

But transport costs are not infinite. International trade does take place. And transport costs are not zero, so that not all goods are freely traded. Samuelson has suggested that the existence of transport costs means that the average proportion of national income earned by exports or spent on imports will be less than 50 per cent.[2] So it is in every case in Table 2–1.[3] This table compares an average of exports and imports with national income. Exports and imports are averaged to eliminate the distortion in those countries that have a large merchandise export surplus because of substantial payments to foreigners on current invisible account, like the earnings of the oil-producing countries; or a large import

---

1959, 4.8 per cent of services consumed were imported, compared with 6.3 per cent of durable and nondurable goods. This calculation excludes construction, of which there are no imports. The 1959 proportion of services to goods was much larger than has been normal because of the high level of services provided to United States military forces abroad. The data are calculated from Table 66 of the Department of Commerce *Survey of Current Business* (July 1960), p. vii–5. For a discussion of world trade in services, see E. Devons, "World Trade in Invisibles," *Lloyds Bank Review*, n.s., *60* (1961), 37–50.

2. Paul A. Samuelson, "The Transfer Problem and Transport Costs: The Terms of Trade When Impediments Are Absent," *Economic Journal, 62* (1952), 290 ff.

3. The Luxembourg national-income accounts (International Monetary Fund, *International Financial Statistics,* August 1960, p. 60) give exports and imports of goods and services each larger than national income. In 1958 national income amounted to 16.7 billion francs, whereas exports were 17.5 billion and imports 17.3 billion. But exports and imports were both smaller than gross national product, at 21.8 billion. The fact seems to be that Luxembourg sells abroad most of what it produces (largely to Belgium), including a very high proportion of services, and purchases abroad virtually all of its consumption and investment, including depreciation. But this is a most exceptional case of a very small country intimately linked to another.

TABLE 2–1. *Foreign Trade as a Percentage of National Income, 1958 (foreign trade equals average of merchandise exports and imports)*

Country	*Percentage*	*Country*	*Percentage*
Iraq (1956)	47	United Kingdom (1959)	20
Netherlands (1959)	45	Western Germany	19
Eire	44	Portugal	19
Iceland[a]	41	Italy	18
Cuba	37	Thailand[b]	18
Belgium[b]	36	Australia (year ended June 30, 1959)	17.5
Venezuela	35	China (Taiwan)[a]	17
Ceylon	34	Colombia	17
Norway	33	Ecuador	17
Denmark	32	Egypt (1956)[b]	17
Ghana[b]	29	Israel	17
Peru (1957)	29	Paraguay	17
Costa Rica	28	Greece	16
New Zealand	27	Chile[a]	14
Austria (1959)	26	France	12.5
Finland	25	Argentina	12
Switzerland	25	Mexico	11.5
Honduras (1957)	23	Philippines	11
Burma (year ended Sept. 30, 1958)	22	Brazil (1959)	9
Guatemala	22	South Korea	9
Canada	21	Pakistan	8
Sweden	21	India	7.5
Panama	20	United States (1959)	4

[a]Goods and services reduced by 10 per cent.

[b]Gross national product reduced by 10 per cent.

Source: Derived from *International Financial Statistics* (August 1960).

Note: This table was derived from statistics of averaged, unadjusted merchandise exports and imports, and national income. Since the figures for trade and income are not strictly comparable, the percentages furnish only an order of magnitude. Where current-account data on trade in goods and services were available in the national-income accounts but not in unadjusted merchandise trade, the former were reduced by 10 per cent to eliminate services roughly. Similarly, a crude adjustment was made to derive a national-income figure, where the source furnished surplus on merchandise-trade account, because of capital imports or because of a substantial earning on the export of services, as in the case of Norway and its shipping.

There are evidently many factors other than transport costs that affect the proportion of foreign trade to national income, for the range is wide between Iraq's 47 per cent and the United States' 4 and the Soviet Union's 2.5. One of the most important of these is size, which we shall discuss presently; the others will be addressed, at greater length, in Chapters 3 to 9.

Transport costs not only exist, but fall into a complex pattern. Space does not permit a detailed exposition of their structure, but the cost of shipping an article from one country to another may be said to depend on a number of considerations: its weight, bulk, value, physical characteristics, the distance to be traversed, the mode and speed of transport, the character of the route, the existence of other cargoes going between the same points, especially in the opposite direction, and so on. Weight and value are among the most important aspects, and a high score on the first combined with a low one on the second is usually sufficient to eliminate a commodity from international trade—unless, to be sure, it can travel almost as ballast in a ship that makes the bulk of

---

only one for gross national product. A number of countries reported on by the International Monetary Fund had to be omitted from the table for lack of the national-income estimate, one for foreign trade in local currency, or the gross foreign trade figures in the income account. Still other countries, like the Soviet Union, are not members of the International Monetary Fund and do not furnish it trade data. Holzman has estimated Soviet exports in 1959 at between 2.3 and 2.6 per cent of national income: "International Trade and Economic Growth: The Soviet Union (1917–1957) and the United States (1869–1913)" (unpublished paper for the Social Science Research Council Conference, Princeton, May 1961).

its profit from transporting cargo in the opposite direction, in which case it becomes the beneficiary of a so-called "back-haul rate." In distance, it is important to emphasize that it is economic distance, not physical, that counts. Thus Argentina and Chile have a common border but limited trade—only 2 per cent of Argentine imports come from Chile, and 4 per cent of Chilean imports from Argentina, compared to such percentages as 18 per cent for the Netherlands from Belgium-Luxembourg and 16 per cent in the opposite direction. The Andes are a formidable barrier to the transport of goods. Similarly, the physical nearness of Austria and Switzerland does not mean economic propinquity because of the Alps, which lie on both sides of the border and separate the major centers of economic activity.

Unfortunately there have been few studies of the structure of transport costs in international trade. One or two conventional rules have been worked out to convert values at the port of export (f.o.b. or free on board) to value at the border of the importing country (c.i.f. or cost, insurance, and freight), or vice versa. Thus it is customary to use an adjustment factor of 5 per cent in intra-European trade and 10 per cent in intercontinental trade (sometimes 15 per cent before World War II). But these rules of thumb ignore, as doubtless they must, the complexity of transport costs and their change over time. Something of this complexity is perhaps conveyed by the material extracted from a report of the United States Tariff Commission on transport costs as a percentage of the import value of particular commodities in 1938. The data relate to imports only, for a particular country and for a year that was not very representative of the price of commodities or freight rates for goods moved by tramp steamer. For what they are worth as a very rough guide, however, they are set out in Table 2–2.

TABLE 2–2. *Relation of Freight to Value of Leading United States Imports, 1938 (freight cost calculated on a net weight basis)*

Commodity	*Supplier*	*Percentage*
Iron ore	Chile	255
Cement	Belgium	78
Bauxite	Surinam	43
Iron ore	Sweden	36
Molasses	Cuba	32
Crude petroleum	Netherlands West Indies	26
Anthracite coal	United Kingdom	26
Oil cake	Philippines	24
Crude petroleum	Venezuela	22
Sodium nitrate	Chile	21
Coconut oil	Philippines	19
Manganese ore	U.S.S.R.	18
Standard newsprint paper	Canada	10–25
Glass	Belgium	17
Bottled wine	Italy	16
Potassium chloride	Germany	16
Cocoa	Ghana	14
Wood pulp	Sweden	9–10
Burlap	India	9
Tuna	Japan	9
Whisky	United Kingdom	8
Coffee	Brazil	8
Tulip bulbs	Netherlands	7
Cotton cloth	Japan (Atlantic Coast)	7
Flaxseed	Argentina	6–8
Cane sugar	Cuba	6
Tea	India	5
Lead bullion	Mexico	5
Steel bars	Belgium	1–9
Carpet wool	Argentina	4
Raw cotton (long staple)	Egypt	4
Rubber	Malaya	4
Aluminum	Norway	3–4
Hops	Czechoslovakia	3
Copper, unmanufactured	Chile	3
Tin	Malaya	3
Cotton cloth	Japan (Pacific Coast)	3

(*Continued overleaf*)

TABLE 2–2 (*continued*)

Commodity	*Supplier*	*Percentage*
Raw silk	Japan (Atlantic Coast)	3
Woolens	United Kingdom	2–4
Cotton cloth	United Kingdom	1–4
Cigar filler and wrapper	Cuba	1
Coal-tar dyes	Germany	1
Razor-blade and other high-grade steel strip	Sweden	1
Raw silk	Japan (Pacific Coast)	1

Source: United States Tariff Commission, *Transportation Costs and Value of Principal Imports* (Washington, D.C., G.P.O., 1940).

Note: H. F. Karreman, who is studying the structure of transport costs in world trade, has published some preliminary results for 1953 in *Methods for Improving World Transportation Accounts, Applied to 1950–1953,* National Bureau of Economic Research, Technical Paper 15 (New York, 1961). Table 5 (pp. 14–15) gives freight rates in terms of percentages of the c.i.f. value for a number of bulky commodities ranging from 71.5 per cent for fuel oil from Indonesia to the Netherlands, through a number of items of coal, fertilizer, crude petroleum, and iron ore at 20 to 30 per cent, and, finally, to wheat, lumber, and sugar at 7 to 10 per cent. Karreman's estimates of freight on imports as a percentage of total c.i.f. import values range from 10 to 12 per cent for countries such as Jordan, Taiwan, Israel, Spain, and Argentina to 5 to 6 per cent for Netherlands overseas territories, Colombia, Iran, Finland, Austria, and Switzerland, to 3.2 per cent for Mexico.

In general, manufactures, including even bulky and heavy manufactures such as machine tools, are readily traded on a world basis. Their transport costs amount to perhaps 2 per cent of delivered value, and can safely be ignored by economists. For primary production, the case is otherwise. Commodities that are sufficiently valuable in relation to their bulk and weight, like cotton and wool, move freely over the face of the entire globe. It is remarkable, for example, that wool is shipped 14,000 miles from Australia to Britain, and 14,000 miles back again in the form of cloth, and that the difference in manufacturing costs of cloth between Britain and

Australia is sufficiently wide to outweigh the costs of the round trip. Refined metals, except for crude steel, are likewise relatively "footloose." But for ores, coal, oil, grains, and heavy bulk commodities like cement, limestone, phosphates, and so on, the costs of transport must be calculated closely.

In some instances these products can move only in limited areas. United States coal exports used to be restricted to the Western Hemisphere, and even now they compete most effectively with European supplies at the extremities—in Italy, Norway, and even Germany, at Hamburg, which is a considerable distance from the Ruhr. Not infrequently a large country will both export and import the same commodity—Canada exports oil to the United States in the Middle West and on the West Coast, while importing it from the Caribbean to the eastern provinces; Germany exports steel to Northern France from the Ruhr and imports it in the South from Lorraine.

As we shall presently see, the steady decline in transport costs relative to costs of production has continuously widened the range of international commodity exchanges and brought into intercontinental trade heavy or bulky products which had previously been traded only over short distances. But transport costs continue to exist, so that not all goods are traded, and they are well below infinity, so that international trade covers a wide range of commodities.

THE ECONOMIC HORIZONS OF PRODUCERS AND CONSUMERS

Besides distance, another barrier to trade exists—lack of knowledge. Too often in economic analysis we assume, along with rationality, perfect knowledge, if not perfect foresight. But awareness of trading opportunities is limited, and can be acquired only at a price. In addition to transport, there must be communication. Where communication is lacking, there can be no international trade.

A man may be perfectly rational, but only within a limited horizon. As a consumer, he will normally restrict his expenditures to those goods offered to him through customary channels. As a producer, he will sell his goods typically in a given ambit. Over his horizon there may lie brilliant opportunities to improve his welfare as a consumer or his income as a producer, but unless he is made aware of them, they will avail him nothing.

The cliché concerning the opening of trade is that trade follows the flag (or the missionary's hymnbook, or medical kit). Channels thus opened may be deepened by trade preferences, but there can be little doubt that, even without these, trade moves parallel to the lines of political communication. A dramatic example is furnished by the contrast between Nigerian and French West African trade in 1958 (see Table 2–3).

Of more importance is the example of trade within the British Commonwealth. The Ottawa Agreement of 1932 in-

TABLE 2–3. *Nigerian and French West African Imports, 1958 (by origin, in value and percentage)*

	Value (in millions of dollars)		*Percentage*	
Nigerian imports: Total	467		100	
from the United Kingdom		204		44
from France		7		2
French West African imports: Total	419		100	
from the United Kingdom		10		2
from France		273		65

Source: United Nations, *Direction of International Trade, 1959* (New York, 1960).

creased the tightness of the links of the Commonwealth in trade; but well before that date trade within the Commonwealth had greatly exceeded the proportions which might have been expected on the basis of population, income, distance, or economic complementarity. Data on the percentage distribution of United Kingdom trade over time illustrate this in a rough fashion, as set out in Table 2–4.

TABLE 2–4. *United Kingdom Trade with the Commonwealth and Other Areas, for Selected Years, 1913–1958 (in per cent of value)*

<table>
<tr><th></th><th colspan="5">Exports to</th><th colspan="5">Imports from</th></tr>
<tr><th></th><th>1913</th><th>1928</th><th>1938</th><th>1948</th><th>1958</th><th>1913</th><th>1928</th><th>1938</th><th>1948</th><th>1958</th></tr>
<tr><td>Commonwealth</td><td>37</td><td>45</td><td>45</td><td>53</td><td>50</td><td>25</td><td>29</td><td>40</td><td>42</td><td>47</td></tr>
<tr><td>United States</td><td>6</td><td>6</td><td>7</td><td>4</td><td>3</td><td>18</td><td>16</td><td>13</td><td>9</td><td>9</td></tr>
<tr><td>Europe</td><td rowspan="2">57</td><td rowspan="2">49</td><td>29</td><td>25</td><td>27</td><td rowspan="2">57</td><td rowspan="2">55</td><td>25</td><td>18</td><td>26</td></tr>
<tr><td>Rest of world</td><td>19</td><td>18</td><td>20</td><td>22</td><td>31</td><td>18</td></tr>
</table>

Sources: For 1913 and 1928: United Kingdom Board of Trade, *Statistical Abstract for the British Empire* (London, 1931). For 1938, 1948, and 1958: United Nations, *Direction of International Trade, 1959.*

Propinquity is, of course, one basis on which knowledge can be acquired, and it eases the maintenance of communication. Travel is facilitated, and it and various other forms of communication—surface and air mail, telegraph, radio, telephone, teletype—are rendered cheaper as well as more expeditious. And yet distance is by no means the only basis for maintaining close ties. It is interesting that the two countries which have the closest trade connections with the United Kingdom—Eire, which sends it 97 per cent of its exports, and New Zealand, which ships 56 per cent—are simultaneously the nearest and the farthest away.

The necessity for establishing and maintaining channels of communication as a prerequisite of trade means that there may be trade opportunities which exist but are not exploited because of lack of knowledge. Most businessmen in the United States "buy American," not out of jingoism, but because similar and cheaper foreign goods have not been brought to their attention. Like the young people in the United States who are bright enough to win scholarships to college but do not go because they never thought of themselves as potential college graduates (or members of the middle class), there are doubtless many trade opportunities frustrated through nothing more than lack of knowledge of or attention to them.

This limitation of the horizon of businessmen and of man in his political capacity is probably an important cause of government intervention in the trade process. Instinctively we feel that a man should take the risks of business competition within his own country. In somewhat technical terms, a man entering a given business should calculate the probability distributions of various events which could affect his success or failure, and should enter the business only if the mean values of the various distributions augur well for success. If he enters the export business, his horizon would of course cover the world of his markets and existing or potential competition abroad. And if he enters competition with existing imports, he should be aware of the range of possible changes among his competitors. But in a purely domestic business, contingencies abroad may typically lie beyond the horizon of the businessman, and a major change in some foreign country which adversely affects his profits will seem unfair because unanticipated. In such cases, businessmen want the government to defend them from what they feel they have no chance to prepare against. The case of competition between the local druggist or grocer and the national chain store is perhaps similar.

With the growth of means of communication and the resulting possibility of rapid and effective transport of goods at great distances, it can be said that the small country provides the businessman with too limited a horizon. Current interest in European economic integration is an expression of this viewpoint. At the same time, however, there must be some limit to the economic horizon that the businessman is asked to scan. It was once suggested to the writer that a "rational man" interested in securities would have subjective estimates of the prices at which he was prepared to buy and sell every security in the world. But this evidently requires operation over an excessively wide horizon. Most businessmen deal in one or a limited number of commodities, and over a limited portion of the earth. If Belgium is too narrow, given the techniques of modern communication, the world is still too broad. It is an administrative principle, as army general staffs and business corporations have found out, that efficiency is enhanced if the scope of a single man's activities is circumscribed. Since businessmen are not capable of operating within a horizon embracing the whole world, there is some use for administrative units, like countries, smaller than the world. It is too much to expect the rational businessman to have in mind prices at which he would buy and sell the commodities which interest him throughout the world, much less that he should interest himself in every commodity everywhere.

Similarly, consumers operate within a horizon, selecting purchases from a limited array of products offered to them, and being strongly affected in tastes by the consumption patterns of the social group to which they belong. An economic change in a foreign country, beyond their horizon, will leave them unaffected for a considerable period. One may even argue that consumers will not feel at all deprived if they fail to get access to a new product developed abroad, or to a cheaper one than the domestic product. At least this is true until the consumers learn about these bargains.

This question of horizon has been put in terms of social groups as far back as the nineteenth-century German economist, Friedrich List: domestic trade is among "us"; foreign trade is between "us" and "them." As communication improves in breadth and speed, the scope of "us" expands. But "they" will probably continue to exist.

TRADE AS A LEARNING PROCESS

There seems a distinct possibility that trade, like many economic processes, follows a learning curve in its development. The import of European automobiles into the United States provides a case in point. Small cars were available in the 1930s, though perhaps not in such effective or inexpensive models as the Volkswagen, the Renault Dauphine, or the Morris Minor. The development of the trade was slow for a time, and then picked up speed, as the figures in Table

TABLE 2–5. *United States Imports of Automobiles, 1953–1959 (by value)*

	Imports (in millions of dollars)	*Percentage of Increase over Previous Year*
1953	55	—
1954	55	0
1955	85	55
1956	145	71
1957	335	130
1958	555	66
1959	845	52

Source: United States Department of Commerce, Bureau of the Census, *United States Imports of Merchandise for Consumption, Commodity by Country of Origin,* Report No. FT 110 (Washington, D.C., G.P.O., various years).

2–5 show. The rate of increase of expansion rose to a peak in 1957 and then declined. Consumers and producers both had to learn of the potentialities of the trade, and it took time to establish dealerships, service and parts, and effective methods of wholesale distribution and transatlantic transport. Of course, there is more to it than this—expansion of production, and possibly a change of tastes. But the learning analogy is a useful one.

TABLE 2–6. *Gross National Product, Industrial Production, and Intracommunity Trade of the European Economic Community, 1953–1959 (in index number, 1953 = 100)*

	Gross National Product	*Industrial Production*	*Intracommunity Trade*
1953	100	100	100
1954	105	110	119
1955	114	122	142
1956	120	132	158
1957	126	140	171
1958	129	144	170
1959	135	153	210

Source: General Agreement on Tariffs and Trade, *International Trade, 1959* (Geneva, 1960), table 43, pp. 148–49.

Ever since the announcement of the establishment of the European Economic Community in 1955, trade among the six members of that customs union has been growing faster than gross national product or industrial production, as Table 2–6 shows. Part of the explanation for this may lie in actual tariff reductions, part in the high income elasticity of demand for imports of industrial products. E.E.C. exports to the largely industrial countries of the European Free Trade Area have also grown more rapidly than gross national product and industrial output in those countries.[4] But part of the faster growth in trade seems to be due to increasing attention within the emerging customs union to the trade opportunities in partner countries. Business opinion is said to have discounted the effects of scheduled decreases in tariffs far in advance of actual reductions, thus rendering obsolete the original timetable of gradual reductions over twelve to fifteen years.[5] While it is not possible to prove it satisfactorily for lack of detailed estimates of income elasticities, this seems to be another case of a change of horizon producing a change in trade.

Trade moves in channels, shaped by the communications network and by transport routes, the latter themselves affected in part by the former. Trade routes lay along Roman roads, and later joined together medieval market towns. The Hanseatic towns developed as centers of trade and of traders. In the eighteenth century there existed a number of trade patterns followed by ships and merchants, such as New England shipments of fish and ice to the West Indies against imports of rum and molasses. The nineteenth century brought the clipper ships and the tea and grain trades. In the second half of the century London became a great entrepôt center, outshining Antwerp, Rotterdam, and Hamburg; and countries such as Sweden and Denmark bought their wool, wheat, tobacco, and leather, not directly from Australia, Canada, the United States, and Argentina, but in the City of London.

Each of these channels developed its own institutions: the

4. E.E.C. exports to E.F.T.A. reached 181 in 1959 on the basis of 1953=100, compared with E.F.T.A. gross national product of 119 and industrial production of 125.

5. But see the doubts of A. Lamfalussy in "Economic Growth and the Common Market," *Lloyds Bank Review* n.s. 62 (1961), 1–16.

merchant trader, the merchant banker, the freight forwarder, the import house, the national corporation. Organized markets developed for standardized goods; and, where standardization and grading could not be accurately achieved because of the fickleness of nature, as in wool, furs, and diamonds, there evolved international auctions with competitive bidding taking place after inspection.

A new era in international trade seems to be arriving with the development of the international corporation—what Maurice Byé calls "the large inter-territorial unit."[6] Made possible by air travel, which provides the necessary face-to-face communication needed to administer complex affairs, with appropriate speed and at a reasonable cost, and by the international telephone, the corporation will expand trade in some directions, perhaps cut it off in others. The movement of technology, administrative capacity, and capital, through the allocating mechanism of the international corporation, may substitute for the physical movement of commodities. But this gets us ahead of our story.

INNOVATIONS IN TRANSPORT

Walter Isard has expressed the idea that innovations in transport have been the major stimulus to world trade.[7] Big reductions have occurred in costs of producing existing goods, as we shall see in Chapter 6, and new goods have been devised and marketed internationally. Such technological

6. "L'Autofinancement de la grande unité interterritoriale et les dimensions temporelles de son plan," *Revue d'économie politique* (1957), translated as "Self-financed Multi-territorial Units and the Time Horizon," International Economic Association, *International Economic Papers, 8* (London, 1958), 147–78.

7. See, for example, "Economic Implications of Aircraft," *Quarterly Journal of Economics, 59* (1945), esp. 145–49.

changes, along with the discovery of natural resources, have been of great importance to world trade. But probably even more important in their influence have been those innovations that have cheapened and sped the movement of goods. There is no need to go back to the Phoenicians and the trireme, nor to the development of the fore-and-aft sails which made square-rigged sailing ships obsolete. The big upsurge in world trade dates from about 1870, when the steam engine was joined to the screw propeller and fitted to the ironclad vessel, to link the continents. The Suez Canal in 1869 connected Asia and Europe; the Panama Canal since 1914 has joined the West Coast of North and South America, Asia, and Oceania to the East Coast of North America and to Europe. The refrigerator ship in the 1880s, the tanker shortly afterward, and lately the international pipeline have continued the process.

As has been discovered many times, a reduction in transport costs may increase profits for the producer at the same time that it lowers prices to the consumer, thereby doubly stimulating the exchange. What the railroad was to do for increased specialization and the development of national markets in England and France, or for transcontinental trade in North America, the development of cheap ocean shipping has done for world trade. New channels of trade have been opened up, new links forged.

There is an element of fixed costs about developing new means of transport, cutting new routes, overcoming barriers to communication, or extending the horizon within which rationality can undertake the maximizing process required by trade. The innovation, or the acquisition of information, involves capital outlays which need not always be repeated. It is true that interference with trade because of war, political revolution, or depression may cause trade channels to silt up and clog, as the ancient ports of Bruges in Belgium and Sète in southern France have become landlocked and isolated from world trade routes. By and large, however, the long-run cost curve of conducting trade is a falling one as the world shrinks in space and time. Trade must overcome distance and barriers to communication, now as before, but the task becomes continuously easier.

3 NATURAL RESOURCES

THE LAW OF COMPARATIVE COSTS

The classic doctrine of international trade, which will occupy us for only a few minutes, states that trade is based on differences in the costs of production of given articles that are wider than their costs of transport in terms of some absolute measure of real cost. These are not absolute differences in costs, but relative, or comparative. It is not necessary for trade that the United States produce electrical machinery more cheaply than Britain, and that Britain produce textiles more cheaply than the United States. If the United States produces both textiles and machinery more cheaply than Britain but its margin of advantage is wider in machinery than in textiles, it will pay to export machinery and import textiles. Sir Donald MacDougall has studied the labor productivities of the United States and Britain over a range of commodities and found that the United States tends to export to Britain those commodities in which its labor productivity is more than twice that of Britain, and to import those in which its labor productivity is less than this multiple.[1]

To what are these cost differences due? The Heckscher-Ohlin theorem, developed by two Swedish economists, asserts that they are due to differences in factor availabilities between countries, on the one hand, and in the factor requirements of different commodities, on the other. Countries with lots of labor will produce cheaply and export labor-intensive commodities; those with lots of land, land-intensive products. And the same for capital.

This formulation assumes that differences in comparative costs will not be offset by differences in tastes between countries. The assumption is pretty well justified by experience. In the absence of trade, differences in comparative costs have to be balanced by differences in consumption patterns. Countries that produce only wheat will eat wheat; those that can grow only rice will eat rice. Some of these consumption patterns will remain permanently embedded in the structure of demand. But when trade is opened up, consumers are likely to alter their tastes because of the opportunity to buy foreign goods. This change, called "demonstration effect"

1. G. D. A. MacDougall, "British and American Exports: A Study Suggested by the Theory of Comparative Costs," pt. I, *Economic Journal, 61* (1951), 697–724; pt. II, *62* (1952), 487–521. This research is theoretically objectionable, both because it uses productivity measures based on a single factor (labor) and ignores the contributions of both natural resources and capital, and because it fails to take into account such land-intensive goods as wheat, cotton, and tobacco and such capital-intensive commodities as chemicals. But within this limitation, and within a restricted range of goods of roughly the same capital–output ratios, it illustrates the law of comparative advantage neatly.

by Professor Nurkse,[2] represents a movement toward establishing the same pattern of tastes in various countries. Differences in taste will remain, based on different cultural patterns and on differences in income, even where the same goods would be consumed at the same level of income. Some trade may even occur because of a preference for foreign goods over cheaper domestic products. But for the most part we can ignore taste as a cause of trade.

Applied to natural resources, the Heckscher-Ohlin theorem states that countries will export the products of natural resources within their borders and import those commodities which require inputs of resources that they lack. To begin with, it must be admitted that it is impossible to measure natural resources in economic terms. Acreage will certainly not suffice as a measure, given the differences between arable, pasture, wooded, and waste land, and, with arable land itself, between plains, rich bottom fields along the rivers, terraced mountainsides, dry lands and those with abundant rainfall. And outside of agriculture and forestry, resources are even more diverse: water-power sites, mineral deposits, natural harbors. Since no standard measure is possible, we cannot say with certainty whether France has more natural resources than Britain, or less, though most observers would intuitively believe the former to be true for agriculture and the latter for industrial resources.

Resources must further be described in relation to a given technology. When the "state of the arts" is altered by innovation, the economic, if not the physical, characteristics of a given resource may change. Improvements in refining methods may make possible the reworking of discarded tailings at depleted mines; new techniques in drilling may extend nat-

2. Ragnar Nurkse, *Some Problems of Capital Formation in Underdeveloped Countries* (Oxford, 1953), p. 58.

ural resources of oil and gas in depth below the earth and extensively into the sea; new seeds may enlarge the area to which a given crop can be planted economically because of better germination or better resistance to heat or frost. Thus, when technology changes, the resource base changes as well.

Not only do resources alter, and remain unmeasurable; frequently natural resources cannot be separated from other factors, and especially from capital. Take two pieces of land of the same size and physical characteristics. One, which originally formed part of an open plain, is a natural resource. Another, which has been cleared of trees, is partly capital. Or suppose that a railroad built into northern British Columbia uncovers mineral deposits. The value of this resource, which previously was uneconomic, can be attributed to the land or to the social overhead capital that connected it to the market and removed it from the category of no-rent land. Land was once described by economists as the indestructible bounty of nature, but conservationists have made clear how destructible land is, and conservation literature tends to divide land into renewable and nonrenewable. Renewable land can be increased or improved by fallowing, fertilization, irrigation. But both kinds of land can be increased by discovery, and by investment which makes no-rent land at the margin more accessible; and both can be decreased by intensive use and depletion. If the discovery of mineral wealth is accidental, then land is land. But if a natural resource is acquired as the result of expensive exploration, it may be regarded as capital. Thus the economist finds himself in initial difficulties of definition and measurement.

RESOURCE SKEWNESS

Every country has to have some resources to be able to exist—a certain minimum of square feet per person, water for drinking, and so on. But above this minimum the Heckscher-Ohlin theorem and the law of comparative advantage presuppose that resources are not neatly matched against a country's requirements. The more skewed—or one-sided—a country's resources are, the more it will trade. This is virtually self-evident. Demand is not likely to be very skewed: there is a minimum of food, clothing, and shelter needed, and above that the law of diminishing returns in consumption ensures that demands will not grow enormously in one direction. If demand covers many commodities, and supply only a few, it is necessary to resort to trade to match the two.

In the early development of trade theory, trade presumably involved the selling of the surplus of some products yielded by a country's resources in exchange for the surplus products of other countries. Adam Smith regarded foreign trade as a "vent for surplus,"[3] evidently presupposing a highly skewed resource base. It is a usual pattern of economic development, widely noted by economists, that countries enter into trade in this fashion by selling abroad the commodities which are "naturally" produced by the resources they have in abundance. Resource skewness produces concentrated trade, of the sort that is frequently found in relatively underdeveloped countries. Part of this concentration may be due to lack of complementary factors required to produce other commodities for which the natural resources exist. We discuss the availability of complementary factors below. In other cases, however, the resource product itself requires large capital investments, frequently from abroad, that are made available only for the resource product. Table 3–1 sets out a list of countries with a concentration of trade of more than 50 per cent in a single export. In most of these countries

3. Hla Myint, "The 'Classical Theory' of International Trade and the Underdeveloped Countries," *Economic Journal, 68* (1958), 321.

TABLE 3–1. *Countries with More than 50 Per Cent of Exports (by Value) in a Single Commodity, 1958*

Country	*Commodity*	*Percentage of Exports in Single Commodity*	*Percentage of National Product Exported*
Mauritius (1957)	Sugar	99	47
Netherlands Antilles	Petroleum	99	—
Iraq	Petroleum	92	—
Venezuela	Petroleum	91	44
Colombia (1957)	Coffee	77	15
Cuba	Sugar	77	35
Burma	Rice	74	21
Haiti	Coffee	74	20
El Salvador	Coffee	73	—
Guatemala	Coffee	73	21
Egypt	Cotton	70	14
Zanzibar	Cloves and clove oil	68	—
Panama	Bananas	67	10
Ceylon	Tea	66	33
Ghana	Cocoa	66	32
Chile	Copper	63	16
Liberia	Rubber	62	—
Malaya	Rubber	62	—
Pakistan	Jute	58	7
Uruguay	Wool	58	—
Bolivia	Tin	57	—
Rhodesia and Nyasaland	Metals	57	35
Ecuador	Bananas	56	20
Ethiopia	Coffee	56	—
Sudan	Cotton	55	—
China (Taiwan)	Sugar	52	14
Honduras (1957)	Bananas	51	22

Sources: International Monetary Fund, *International Financial Statistics,* 1960 issues, except for ratio of exports to national income, of Guatemala, Ghana, and China (Taiwan), computed from United Nations, *Yearbook of National Accounts Statistics, 1959* (New York, 1960).

(those for which data are available) the ratio of export to national income is also high. P. Lamartine Yates observes, moreover, that while the list of one-commodity exporters has changed since 1913, it is getting longer, not shorter.[4]

Skewness of economic capacity, as mentioned, is not exclusively a matter of natural resources. In the first place, capital may be required as a complement to natural resources, as in petroleum mining and refining. Secondly, as we shall see in Chapter 6, capital itself is not a homogeneous and fungible factor, but becomes invested in specific and specialized uses from which it can be withdrawn only slowly over time through the diversion of depreciation allowances, much as depletion allowances may be taken out of a nonrenewable resource and invested in similar or different resources or capital assets. Long-run decreasing costs may be a basis for specialization and trade in an industry requiring skewness of invested capital and even of labor skills. We come to this below. But while we here treat of trade based on skewness of natural resources, it deserves mention that man-made skewness can also serve as a basis for trade.

SKEWNESS AND SIZE

The smaller the economy in geographic area, the more skewed it is likely to be and the more it must trade outside its borders. Conversely, the larger the economy in geographic area, the less skewed and the smaller its trade as a proportion of its income. This is partly due to natural resources. If resources are randomly distributed in space, the larger the geographic area covered by a given political unit, the less specialized will that unit's resources be. Natural resources

4. *Forty Years of Foreign Trade* (London, 1959), p. 180. It should be added that the list of countries is longer, too.

are evidently not distributed entirely at random, but the assumption that they are may serve as a convenient first approximation. It also follows from what has been said about long-run decreasing costs that the larger the country, the more opportunities it will have to achieve an optimum size domestically, without need for foreign trade, in industries which are based not on natural resources but on capital investment and labor skills. But here size is a function of population, rather than geographic area, and, further, the theorem applies only above a certain level of skill and income per capita.

Table 3–2 undertakes to compare population, area, and foreign trade per capita for a number of countries. The countries are ranked in the order of ratio of foreign trade to national income set out in Table 2–1, starting with those with the highest percentage of trade and moving downward. Land is given in total area and with subtraction for built-up land and waste. The table shows that the large countries in both population and land mass have small ratios of foreign trade to national income, even though some, like the United States, have a relatively large dollar amount of trade per capita. At the other end of the scale are the densely populated countries that are small in area, like the Netherlands, Belgium, Denmark, and Norway—the last being small after subtraction of wasteland—and some large countries, like Venezuela and Peru, with a relatively small population. In the middle of the list are two types of countries: the densely populated industrial ones, like Britain and Germany, and the large, lightly populated ones of high income, like Canada, Australia, and New Zealand.

Of course, averages hide significant aspects of the problem. Thus Indonesia, if we had data for it, would produce a single figure averaging the densely populated island of Java, which

TABLE 3–2. *Size, Population, and Foreign Trade Per Capita Compared with Foreign Trade Ratio, Late 1950s*[a]

Country	*Population (in millions)*	*Area*		*Foreign Trade*	
		Total	*Total less Waste and Built-up*	*Dollars Per Capita*	*Ratio to National Income*
		(in thousands of square kilometers)		*(average exports and imports)*	
Iraq	6.6	444.4	202.0	66	47
Netherlands	11.2	32.5	25.7	306	45
Eire	2.9	70.3	47.7	249	44
Iceland	.2	103.0	7.5	450	41
Cuba	6.5	114.5	71.9	115	37
Belgium	9.1	30.5	23.1	342	36
Venezuela	6.3	912.1	367.2	297	35
Ceylon	9.4	65.6	50.5	38	34
Norway	3.5	323.9	69.7	291	33
Denmark	4.5	43.0	35.7	278	32
Ghana	4.8	237.9	205.1	55	29
Peru	10.2	1,285.2	837.3	22	29
Costa Rica	1.1	50.9	16.8	92	28
New Zealand	2.3	268.7	227.7	308	27
Austria	7.0	83.8	70.3	142	26
Finland	4.4	337.0	213.9	172	25
Switzerland	5.2	41.3	30.2	314	25
Honduras	1.8	112.1	78.1	38	23
Burma	20.3	678.0	565.2	10	22
Guatemala	3.5	108.9	66.1	34	22
Canada	17.0	9,974.4	4,159.0	325	21
Sweden	7.4	449.7	230.0	300	21
Panama	1.0	74.5	62.7	58	20
United Kingdom	51.9	244.0	207.1	193	20
Western Germany	52.2	248.0	209.8	157	19
Portugal	9.0	92.2	80.2	43	18
Italy	48.7	301.2	270.9	59	18
Thailand	21.5	514.0	399.2	16	18
Australia	9.8	7,704.2	4,268.2	175	17.5

Natural Resources

Country	Population (in millions)	Area: Total	Area: Total less Waste and Built-up	Foreign Trade: Dollars Per Capita	Foreign Trade: Ratio to National Income
		(in thousands of square kilometers)		(average exports and imports)	
China (Taiwan)	9.9	36.0	26.9	20	17
Colombia	13.5	1,138.4	871.1	32	17
Ecuador	4.0	270.7	253.7	22	17
Egypt	24.8	1,000.0	31.3	24	17
Israel	20.0	20.7	12.6	143	17
Paraguay	1.7	406.8	217.7	20	17
Greece	8.2	132.6	105.8	49	16
Chile	7.3	741.8	291.4	55	14
France	44.6	551.2	504.2	120	12.5
Argentina	20.2	2,778.4	2,395.3	55	12
Mexico	32.3	1,969.3	1,339.4	27	11.5
Philippines	24.0	299.7	275.8	22	11
Brazil	62.7	8,513.8	7,745.8	21	9
South Korea	22.5	96.9	54.6	9	9
Pakistan	85.6	944.8	268.2	4	8
India	397.4	3,263.4	2,424.6	4	7.5
United States	174.8	9,363.4	7,779.1	88	4
U.S.S.R.	208.8	22,403.0	14,713.7	—	—

[a]Latest figures from the sources cited.

Sources: Population: United Nations, *Statistical Yearbook, 1959*. Areas: Food and Agriculture Organization, *Production Yearbook, 1958* (Rome, 1959). Trade: United Nations, *Direction of International Trade, 1958*. Foreign trade ratio: Table 2–1.

has relatively little export trade, with the sparsely settled outer islands, which produce most of the rubber, tea, sugar, and oil. In these cases, with no central tendency, an average is representative of nothing in particular.

But it is evident that size and skewness are related. The most highly specialized unit in a modern economy is the city. If New York City, a developed area, were cut off politically but not economically from its surrounding country, its size would leave it with a very high ratio of exports and imports to income. A country like the Netherlands approaches the concentration of an urban population. At the other end of the scale, the United States and the Soviet Union have very low ratios of exports and imports to income, primarily because of the diversity of resources within their borders.

It seems likely that the north-south extent of an economy is more significant than the east-west, especially if it spreads between the temperate and the tropical zones. There is likely to be some diversity of resources from east to west, but that from north to south is certain. If we assume an average propensity to consume tropical foodstuffs which is the same for all countries of equal income (presupposing something close to similar tastes), it is evident that countries with tropical or semitropical areas within their borders, like the United States and the Soviet Union, will have a lower average propensity to import than countries that lie wholly within the temperate zone.

The line between domestic and foreign trade depends therefore more on the political considerations determining the size of a given country than on economic considerations—or at least in many cases. World trade increased remarkably between 1913 and, say, 1924 for the entirely fictitious reason that the Austro-Hungarian Empire was divided into a series of successor states, trade among which was shifted from the class of domestic to foreign commerce. (The autarchic policies pursued by these states and the reduction of economic interdependence between them produced some slight offset to this statistical "expansion" in trade.) By the same token, we can expect a considerable reduction in world trade, statistically speaking, from the various moves toward economic integration such as customs unions.

European trade does not altogether neglect resource products: Germany exports coal to neighboring countries of Europe; France and Luxembourg, iron ore; France, bauxite; Italy, citrus fruit and sulphur; Germany, Rhine wines; and France, Bordeaux and Burgundy. This trade, which is not small, illustrates that there is a considerable amount of resource skewness not based on size or on any very large differences in latitude. It may be that resources are not distributed randomly between countries on an east-west line since, historically, natural resources have attracted and repelled settlement and have had an influence on the drawing of national boundaries in settlements after wars.[5] But in short-run terms, resource skewness exists independently of national boundaries and is a cause of trade among the most highly developed and industrial countries.

DISCOVERY AND DEPLETION

International trade theory began with the assumption that all factors of production were in fixed supply (and fully employed). It then became evident that capital accumulation and population growth must be taken into account. If capital and labor grow, their factor supplies change relative to each other, unless they proceed at exactly the same rate, and also to land, if that remains fixed. But land does not change in relative fashion alone. Its supply can vary absolutely, even with a fixed technology. Discovery expands natural resources, and depletion contracts them.

5. The German commission detaching Meurthe-et-Moselle from France at the Treaty of Frankfort in 1871 believed that it had included all the major iron as well as coal mines in the ceded territory. But industry discovered new deposits on the French side of the new line.

Much discovery has been accidental. The nickel mines of Sudbury in Canada, which produce between 80 and 90 per cent of the world's supply, were stumbled upon in the course of building the transcontinental railroad. Gold strikes, diamond finds, even the discovery of major oil fields, have been the work of individual prospectors or wildcatters with a small grubstake. But these romantic days are virtually over. Exploration has become scientific, large-scale, based on seismograph and magnometer as well as on surface indications. Each dry hole adds to the total geological picture of the underground structure.

Discovery goes hand in hand with depletion, at least in the middle stages. In a new country, discovery leads; in the older lands, depletion. In the United States, for years, additions to proved reserves of oil just about equaled reserves utilized. But the cost of exploration rose, and this was a sign that depletion was gaining. In economic analysis it is virtually impossible for a country to run out of a good; what happens is that the cost of producing it rises. When the price of exploration goes high enough, it pays to buy the product abroad, or to substitute for it in consumption. When this occurs, it is possible to say that the country has run out of the good in an economic sense, even though in time of need, such as a war, it can increase the output of the commodity markedly.

Depletion has been going on for years in Europe. Lately there have been discoveries too: the gas fields of Lacq in France; the oil fields along the German-Dutch border and in Sicily; the geothermic springs in Central Italy. Iron ore reserves of Lorraine seem expansible without limit, as new fields have been discovered continuously for the last hundred years. By contrast, the tin mines of Cornwall are virtually closed down, although a project to open a new one is discussed from time to time, and many were opened on a limited basis during both world wars; the copper mines of France, too, no longer produce much. But depletion, long thought to have run its course in the most developed continents, seems to have had a new run for its money from discovery.

The most striking discoveries of the last decade, however, have been those of oil in North Africa—the Sahara and Libya. The economic justification of this exploration effort is questionable, but the oil will flow in international trade anyway. The French, long sensitive to the fact that Anglo-Dutch-American interests dominate world oil, have been exploring vigorously within their areas of political dominance. The efforts of French geologists and oil companies have been motivated not only by the desire to match the exploits of the oil "cartel" and to bring glory to France, but also by the need for fuel, and by the importance after World War II of conserving foreign exchange. But these economic reasons are inadequate. What matters is not having oil in one's territory —except during a wartime or siege economy—but getting it cheaply. The German balance of payments has not suffered, it would seem, from the fact that the economy buys its oil from foreign companies.[6] Some French business (possibly antigovernment) circles believe that Saharan oil is expensive, and that France would have been better advised to have used

6. This is not the place to raise the question whether the seven Anglo-Dutch-American oil companies constitute a world cartel, as the United States Federal Trade Commission holds (see *Report* of the United States Senate Small Business Committee, Subcommittee on Monopoly, Washington, D.C., August 1952), or whether the price of oil in Europe has been too high, as the Economic Commission for Europe has suggested (see United Nations Economic Commission for Europe, "The Price of Oil in Western Europe," Geneva, 1955, mimeographed). These issues are reserved for brief discussion in chap. 8.

its resources in producing other goods for export, or other goods to replace imports, thus enabling the economy to acquire fuel more cheaply. This is the essence of the law of comparative advantage. It is a mistake to exploit oil merely because it has been discovered, if its cost is high and the economy can obtain the equivalent elsewhere at lower long-run cost.

But to return to depletion. The tin mines of Cornwall and the copper mines of France may symbolize depletion in Europe, but the most thoroughgoing impact of depletion on the pattern of world trade has been that experienced by the United States. In 1850 the country was a resource-oriented, primary-product country, whose exports were dominated by farm products and minerals. In the 1950s and 1960s it imported on balance every mineral in the list, except two: coal and molybdenum. The ranks of former export products which have shifted to an import basis include silver, lead, zinc, copper, oil, iron ore, and aluminum. Table 3–3 shows that much of the financial impact of this shift occurred after World War II; exports of minerals and mineral products, including coal and lubricating oil, rose sharply; but imports,

TABLE 3–3. *United States Net Trade in Minerals and Metals, 1936–1955 (five-year annual averages, in millions of dollars)*

	Exports	*Imports*	*Net Exports (— = net imports)*
1936–40	820	366	454
1941–45	1,397	756	641
1946–50	1,749	1,423	326
1951–55	2,135	2,887	−752

Source: Statistical Abstract of the United States, 1958, (Washington, D.C., G.P.O., 1958) tables 1138, 1139, pp. 882–84: groups 5 (nonmetallic minerals) and 6 (metals and manufactures), the latter after subtraction of finished iron and steel and finished manufactures.

especially of crude petroleum and residual fuel oil, rose even faster, with the swing in the balance from an export to an import basis of more than a billion dollars in annual average between 1946–50 and 1951–55. Table 3–4 shows in broad terms over a longer period the percentage decline of crude

TABLE 3–4. *The Structure of United States Exports and Imports, 1820–1959*
(percentage breakdown by broad commodity classes)

	Crude Materials and Foodstuffs		*Manufactured Foodstuffs and Semimanufactures*		*Finished Manufactures*	
	Exports	*Imports*	*Exports*	*Imports*	*Exports*	*Imports*
1820	65	16	29	27	6	57
1850	68	18	19	28	13	55
1861–70	54	26	29	23	16	41
1881–90	54	37	30	22	16	31
1901–10	42	46	33	22	26	25
1921–25	37	49	26	31	36	21
1926–30	31	49	24	29	45	22
1936–40	23	46	25	35	52	19
1946–50	22	49	21	33	57	18
1956–59	20	38	21	33	59	30

Source: Statistical Abstract of the United States, 1955, p. 903; *1960*, p. 1189.

manufactures and foodstuffs in United States export trade, and the rise in imports along with the rising and declining shares of finished manufactures in exports and imports, respectively. Note again that this depletion and change of comparative advantage may be relative, not absolute. The oil industry in the United States has been increasing its absolute output from year to year, with occasional setbacks, while its relative share of United States consumption has been declining. This is because domestic output cannot keep up with the demand for oil, as affected by the growth of population and the rise in per capita income. Of course domestic production has been sustained, and demand perhaps slightly checked, by the restrictions on imports which have kept internal prices in the United States well above the world price.

THE AVAILABILITY OF COMPLEMENTARY RESOURCES

Resources are not enough to produce primary products which may be exported, but must be combined with other factors of production. Immigration into the empty lands of the Western Hemisphere and Oceania was necessary before these lands could spill forth their surplus of resource products for the Old World. In peopled areas, such as the Middle East, Asia, and Africa, it is often not labor that is needed as much as capital, organization, and access to markets. These were seldom locally available when the growth of world trade got under way in the middle of the nineteenth century, and had to be provided from Europe or the United States. Tropical lands produced sugar, coffee, rubber, bananas, pineapples in small quantities through the bounty of nature; but making these crops available in substantial amounts and in the standardized product demanded by distant markets required plantations. Oil in the ground in the Middle East was worthless without the technology, capital, and markets possessed solely by foreigners. Frequently it was necessary to build ports, roads, towns, schools, in addition to wells, tanks, terminals, and refineries. Dividing the benefits of the resultant productivity between the foreigners, on the one hand, and the local factors of production, on the other, became an increasingly complex and difficult task as local forces gained understanding of the economic process, appetite for income, and competence in modern technology.

The distribution of tasks and income is complicated further by elements of national feeling and pride. To supply only the labor, and none of the direction and management, is thought to involve the consignment of local people to an inferior position. In the view of some, it is not the distribution of income to cooperating factors which raises the most prickly questions, as much as the sense of the local peoples that they are not managing their own affairs.

TABLE 3–5. *The Structure of Canadian Exports, 1868–1958 (percentage breakdown by broad commodity classes)*

Period	*Raw Materials*	*Manufactured Foodstuffs and Semimanufactures*	*Finished Manufactures*
1868–70	95		5
1876–80	94		6
1886–90	95		5
1896–1900	92		8
1906–10	89		11
1914	87		13
1921	44	32[a]	24
1926–29	47	30	23
1936–39	32	40	28
1946–49	27	28	45
1956–58	33	30	37

[a]Manufactures of farm origin, rather than manufactured food.

Sources: 1886–1914: *Canada Year Book, 1915* (Ottawa, 1916); 1921: ibid., *1930* (Ottawa, 1931); 1926–58: ibid., *1960* (Ottawa, 1961).

Perhaps the most interesting case is that of Canada, which is a major producer of primary products, fully developed, but which nonetheless feels uneasy as it contemplates its role as a purveyor of resource products. Table 3–5 shows that Canada's export structure has changed less in the direction of exports of manufactured goods than has that of the United States.[7] Canada's policy has always been to encourage and

7. For a discussion, see David W. Slater, "Changes in the Structure of Canada's International Trade," *Canadian Journal of Economic and Political Science, 21* (1955), 1–19.

assist the exploitation of its natural resources. Tariffs on manufactured goods were levied after Confederation in 1869, and steps have been taken by the provinces to encourage the processing of pulpwood into wood pulp within their boundaries. But Canada has never undertaken to differentiate between domestic and foreign entrepreneurship in the resource industries.[8] Dominion and provincial governments have consistently encouraged exploration for and exploitation of natural resources—by depletion allowances in taxation, as in the United States, and even by providing social overhead capital in the form of roads to make the wilderness accessible to private investors. But despite the fact that this policy has paid well, Canadians are restive. A Royal Commission on Canada's Economic Prospects discarded a view produced in a staff study which suggested that if American businessmen maximize profits and Canadian businessmen maximize profits, American businessmen in Canada will act in the same way, and with the same economic results, as Canadian businessmen. The Commission recommended some mild steps calling for registration of foreign entrepreneurs, publicity for company reports, more appointments of Canadian directors and hiring of Canadian top staff, and requirements that stock be made available to Canadian investors.[9]

When they acquire capital through saving or borrowing, most countries are anxious to develop capital-intensive industries as rapidly as possible. But the necessity to rely on foreign capital in many resource industries must be recognized; and the Canadian success in investing governmental

8. Such a country as Norway, for example, forbids foreigners to own mining concessions, on the ground that the natural resources of the country are an inalienable asset of Norwegian citizens.

9. Royal Commission on Canada's Economic Prospects, *Final Report* (Ottawa, 1957), pp. 393 ff.

capital not in capital-intensive industries, or even in resource industry, but in social overhead capital that is complementary to foreign investments in resource industries, may well be worth attention. It nonetheless disturbs even the sophisticated Canadians.

TRANSPORT COSTS AND INTERMEDIATE GOODS

It used to be said that a country had to have domestic supplies of rich iron ore and coking coal before it could have a steel industry. Latin America's economic future was thought dim for lack of coal. Japan was believed condemned to a low standard of living because it lacked basic resources. France complained all through the nineteenth century and well into the twentieth that it lacked the rich supplies of coal enjoyed by Britain. Britain complains today that it is unable to feed itself, and that it lacks the resource ingredients of a continental nation, especially those of oil, rich iron ore, and nonferrous metals. Germany complained after the Potsdam Agreement in 1945 that it had been cut off from its breadbasket in the east—East Prussia, Pomerania, Brandenburg, and Mecklenburg.

It is true that abundant and varied resources are necessary for an economy under siege; that Japan, Britain, and Western Germany are not well equipped to feed themselves during a war, nor Argentina and Venezuela to provide themselves with heavy steel products. But more and more, as transport costs fall, dependence on domestic supplies of resource goods is of no peacetime consequence. New York City is perhaps the richest area in the world and has a poor resource base (in goods, not in its harbor or location). Hong Kong imports even its drinking water. Japan is finding that it can "add value" to imported raw materials, even heavy ones like iron ore and coking coal; obtain the resource products it needs for its own consumption; and even export some at a not very advanced level of fabrication. Resources are highly specialized. But like many specialized products of great utility, they can be acquired by exchange, and are not vital.

There are many extreme ideas on the role of resources in the good life. On the one hand, there is the belief that abundant resources are necessary to a high standard of living, like that of the United States. This is not so. Look at Britain, or Switzerland, or even Western Germany, which experienced a gain from the loss of the inefficient agriculture of Eastern Germany, and would be still better off if its peasant areas in the west could be drastically reorganized into larger-scale, mechanized units, since as presently organized they are a serious drag on its level of living.[10] On the other hand, it is frequently claimed that specialization in resource products is ruinous. This is not true. Regard Canada, not to mention Australia, New Zealand, Denmark, most of which are transforming themselves into industrial countries by means of the wealth produced from resources.

One can summarize only by a series of banalities: some resources are better than others; resources are neither necessary nor sufficient for a high level of living; other things equal, more resources are better than fewer resources; but other things unequal, capital, technology, and capacity to transform may be better than some resources. But this last thought must wait for development below.

10. Theodore W. Schultz, "Effects of Trade and Industrial Output of Western Germany upon Agriculture," *American Economic Review, Papers and Proceedings, 40* (1950), 522–30; and H. H. Liesner, *The Import Dependence of Britain and Western Germany: A Comparative Study* (Princeton, 1957).

4 LABOR

THE LABOR THEORY OF VALUE

The law of comparative costs was originally set out by Ricardo in terms of the labor theory of value. All costs were expressed in terms of days of labor required to produce various goods. Casks of wine and bolts of cloth cost so-and-so many days to produce in Portugal, and so-and-so many in England. Relative differences in these costs opened up the possibility of profitable trade.

The labor theory of value relied on constant costs. Men could be shifted from the production of one good to another in unlimited numbers without changing the cost of production in man-days per unit. The theory disregarded the contribution of other factors of production. To achieve differences in costs for a given commodity between countries, the classical economists had to assume either that men were different in skills or other attributes from one country to another, or that they worked with intangible differences in climate or atmosphere. Man-made differences in skills—the result of training or education which could be ascribed to additional inputs—had to be ignored, along with differences in natural resources and capital supply.

Taussig took this theory further and connected it with money wage rates. Wages were a function of the productivity of labor in different countries. The vulgar "cheap labor" argument of the businessman was wrong: one country could not outsell another in every line of endeavor based on cheaper wages, because exports would exceed imports, gold would be acquired, wages would rise in the low-wage country, and fall in the high-wage country. Wages could remain lower in one country than another only as a result of basic differences in productivity, the reasons for which were largely ignored.

Modern economics is unable to accept the labor theory of value. In the first place, no factor of production, including labor, is homogeneous. As more of a factor is added to the production of a given output, costs per unit rise. (We ignore long-run decreasing costs for the time being.) In addition, land and capital cannot be overlooked. The law of variable proportions states that factors can be combined in various ways to produce the same output, and that the more abundant and cheaper a given factor is, the more of it will be used.

THE LABOR-SCARCE ECONOMY

In the Heckscher-Ohlin theorem, the existence of factor endowments varying from one country to another is combined with the fact that production functions of commodities typically require skewed inputs of factors, to suggest that a country's exports and imports will be determined by its factor endowment. A country which is long on resources and short on labor will export resource-intensive products and import labor-intensive goods.

Stolper and Samuelson proved what Australian economists had observed intuitively—that imports of labor-intensive products reduced the return to labor in importing countries such as Australia and the United States.[1] Imports increased the supply of labor-intensive goods, lowered their price, decreased their production, and released labor in greater proportions than they released other factors, to compete on domestic factor markets. Assuming that exports rise with imports, and consist of resource-intensive goods, the price and production of land-intensive goods and the demand for land relative to that for other factors all rise. With perfect factor markets, the price of land rises and the price of labor falls—in every occupation. Thus trade raises the price of the abundant factor, and lowers that of the scarce. By analogous reasoning, a tariff, or any other action that reduces trade, will reduce the return to the abundant factor and raise that of the scarce.

The possibility of international factor movements, ignored by the classical economists, somewhat alters this picture. Some commodities, like cotton, demanded both a special type of land and large amounts of labor. The institution of slavery in America made possible the export of cotton in the 1830s and 1840s to feed the rising demand emanating originally from Britain's Lancashire but ultimately from France, the United States, and Japan. When the Civil War cut off the

1. W. F. Stolper and P. A. Samuelson, "Protection and Real Wages," *Review of Economic Studies, 9* (1941), 58–73, reprinted in American Economic Association, *Readings in the Theory of International Trade* (Homewood, Ill., 1949).

United States supply from the mills of the world, Egypt and India with their truly labor-intensive economies turned to the production of cotton for world markets, to be followed in the twentieth century by less labor-intensive countries, such as Brazil and Peru. With the abolition of slavery in America, wage rates for agricultural labor in the South rose but slowly, and picked up only when the world wars led to the large-scale movement of labor to the North and capital to the South, to erode the supply of Negro labor available at a subsistence level of wages. Cotton growing responded by changing its location, its factor proportions, and its technology, to maintain its position as an export commodity. The story is a highly involved one, and it is necessary to disregard much significant detail in a brief account, including particularly agricultural policies on price supports and export subsidies. But in effect, cotton has become, like wheat, more a capital-intensive than a labor- and land-intensive product. Its center of production has moved relentlessly from the Georgia and Alabama area to Mississippi, and then to the Southwest. Irrigation (capital) now regulates the humidity of growing conditions, and cultivation and harvesting are undertaken on enormous farms by machinery (again capital). More and more, the plantation is being operated as a single, large-scale unit, frequently under corporate management, instead of being broken up into a large number of sharecropper subunits, farmed on the basis of relatively primitive, labor-intensive techniques.

Other labor-intensive commodities that survived in the United States originally owing to slavery, like rice and sugar in Louisiana, or with protection, like sugar beets in Utah, have become capital-intensive. The most striking example is perhaps rice, which is sown from airplanes and harvested by motorboat. This contrasts sharply with the primitive East

Indian method of broadcast sowing, and the peculiarly labor-intensive Japanese method of rooting each plant by hand.

But to return to factor movements: as empty economies, Australia and Canada have viewed the tariff as a means of raising the return to labor to encourage immigration. The theory of international trade has taken the law of variable factor proportions and used it to illustrate how, under particular circumstances, when goods move and factors cannot, goods may substitute for factor movements in bringing about the equalization of factor returns between countries.[2] But by the same token, interference with the movement of goods can encourage the movement of factors.[3]

THE LABOR-INTENSIVE ECONOMIES

In the previous chapter, Japan was cited as a country with a very low land–labor ratio which survived by importing raw materials and exporting finished goods. Its contribution, in value added, has traditionally come from labor-intensive processing. Its major export in the 1920s, silk—which was also the leading import commodity of the United States in terms of value in 1929—was a peculiarly labor-intensive product, requiring feeding silkworms with mulberry leaves, on the one hand, and tedious gathering and processing of the fiber, on the other. Other Japanese exports of the period—cotton textiles and notions, such as cheap toys—also required massive inputs of cheap labor. Today Japan has

2. There is an enormous literature on this subject. The interested student will find it noted and discussed in Richard E. Caves, *Trade and Economic Structure: Models and Methods* (Cambridge, Mass., 1960), chap. 3.

3. This has been demonstrated for capital by Robert A. Mundell, "International Trade and Factor Mobility," *American Economic Review*, 47 (1957), 321–35.

substantially altered the structure of its foreign trade; and the position of the leading economy with a flourishing foreign trade based on cheap labor goes to Hong Kong, with India trailing behind. Cut off by the Cold War but a potential exporter of labor-intensive products is mainland China. And a further economy which has attempted to use its abundant population (along with its position in the United States customs area and its special tax advantage) to attract labor-intensive industry from the United States is Puerto Rico.

The view of the American or British textile manufacturer is that he faces hopeless odds vis-à-vis his oriental competitor who pays his labor a "bowl of rice a day" or "14 cents an hour against our rates of $2.31," or whatever the figures may be said to be. The matter is complex. In the first place, one must consider not only wage rates but labor costs, which depend on labor efficiency as well. It has often been observed that low-wage labor is not necessarily cheap in terms of efficiency. Much depends on whether the labor is disciplined to the tempo of factory work, whether absenteeism is low or high, and even whether the workers are sufficiently nourished to be able to meet the physical demands of their employment.

Secondly, as observed, labor is not the only factor of production. In 1953 when United States businessmen were envying the West Germans their abundant supplies of cheap, efficient labor, continuously increased by the stream of refugees from the East, the German economic press was full of complaints of the *Kapital Knappheit* or capital shortage, with its scarcity and high cost for capital, so abundant in the United States. (Today the scarcity of capital and the abundance of labor have both eased up in Western Germany, but the former perhaps more than the latter.) Similarly, United States steel manufacturers regard themselves as handicapped by the high wages obtained by the unions in their industry, as compared with the wage rates of, say, Belgium, while Belgian manufacturers of steel wish they could obtain cheap supplies of coking coal, abundant in the United States.

But there is evidently something to the view that a flourishing export trade can be built on the basis of cheap (and efficient) labor. The economic literature of the 1920s, as that of today, suggests that a country's relative position in foreign trade depends on whether the commodities it produces for export are in rising or falling demand—whether, that is, its exports enjoy high income-elasticity in a world of rising per capita income, or are old-line, standardized, staple articles, perhaps even inferior goods, the consumption of which decreases as income rises. In the interwar period, the German University of Kiel published the results of a broad investigation (the Enquête Ausschuss), concluding that the United States' gains in international trade had been based on the fact that its exports had been largely goods of high income-elasticity of demand—automobiles, agricultural machinery, radios, etc. Germany had done fairly well because of machinery and electrical goods, despite the existence of a few items in its export list, like pianos and embroidery, that were losing ground. But Britain, with its strong specialization in cotton textiles, was slipping badly. What counted was structure.[4]

This view attracted much attention in the 1920s, as it does today, with economists interested in economic development. But a young economist, H. Tsyzynski, pointed out in a brilliant article that the Enquête Ausschuss statistical investiga-

4. Institut für Weltwirtschaft und Seeverkehr an der Universität Kiel, *Der Deutsche Aussenhandel unter der Einwirkung weltwirtschaftlicher Strukturwandlungen*, 2 (Vol. 20 of the *Ausschuss zur Untersuchung der Erzeugnungs—und Absatzbedingungen der Deutschen Wirtschaft*, Berlin, 1932), esp. pp. 156 ff.

tion left out the case of Japan.[5] He suggested that there were two major influences to be taken into account in evaluating the export performance of a country over time: the structural

TABLE 4–1. *Hypothetical and Actual Shares of World Export Trade in Manufactures, 1899 and 1937*

	Actual Share		*Hypothetical*	*Changes in Percentage Share*		
	1899	*1937*	*Share, 1937*[a]	*Due to Competition*	*Due to Structure*	*Total*
Japan	1.5	7.2	1.0	+6.2	−0.5	+5.7
Canada	0.3	5.0	0.5	+4.5	+0.2	+4.7
United States	11.2	19.6	16.2	+3.4	+5.0	+8.4
Sweden	1.0	2.5	1.3	+1.2	+0.3	+1.5
Italy	3.7	3.6	2.6	+1.0	−1.1	−0.1
India	2.3	2.1	1.7	+0.4	−0.6	−0.2
Belgium	5.6	5.9	5.7	+0.2	+0.1	+0.3
Germany	22.2	22.4	22.6	−0.2	+0.4	+0.2
Switzerland	3.9	2.9	3.3	−0.4	−0.6	−1.0
France	15.8	6.4	14.2	−7.8	−1.6	−9.4
United Kingdom	32.5	22.4	31.0	−8.6	−1.5	−10.1
Total	100.0	100.0	100.0	Net 0	0	0

[a]Table assumes that the trade of each country had grown in each class in the same degree as the trade of all countries combined in that class.

Source: H. Tsyzynski, "World Trade in Manufactured Commodities, 1899–1950," *Manchester School of Economic and Social Studies, 19* (1951), 289.

effect, of which the Enquête Ausschuss had made so much, and the competitive effect. The structural effect could be measured between two dates by calculating the gain in trade which the country would have registered if it had experi-

5. "World Trade in Manufactured Commodities, 1899–1950," *Manchester School of Economic and Social Studies, 19* (1951), 289.

enced, in each broad class of manufactures, the same gain or loss as the class as a whole. But the competitive effect remained, and accounted for the difference between the hypothetical performance, based on structure, and the actual results. Table 4–1 shows that while Britain was a loser in world trade between 1899 and 1937, because of the structure

TABLE 4–2. *Share of World Trade Gained or Lost in Each Group of Manufactured Exports, 1899–1937*

Expanding Groups	*Japan*	*United Kingdom*
Motor vehicles	+1.8	−6.6
Industrial equipment	+2.7	−18.1
Iron and steel	+3.2	−29.4
Electrical goods	+3.8	−10.7
Subtotal	+2.7	−22.9
Stable Groups		
Miscellaneous materials	+3.4	+2.1
Nonferrous metals	−2.6	−2.1
Chemicals	+1.6	−5.4
Agricultural equipment	+0.3	−22.7
Metal manufactures	+4.2	−6.8
Books, films, etc.	+6.8	+6.9
Nonmetalliferous	+5.8	+4.4
Subtotal	+2.6	−2.6
Declining Groups		
Drink and tobacco	+1.4	+26.9
Railway equipment, ships	+5.9	−27.9
Miscellaneous manufactures	+11.0	+3.8
Apparel	+21.3	−1.6
Textiles	+16.8	−8.8
Subtotal	+14.7	−5.4
Total	+6.2	−8.6

Source: same as for Table 4–1, p. 290.

of its trade, and the United States a gainer, Japan made a large overall gain despite a structural loss. And Japan's gains, as Table 4–2 shows, were largely recorded in the declining classes.

Textiles are widely regarded as a peculiarly labor-intensive commodity. But this is a vast oversimplification. Even in cotton textiles, and without going further afield into woolens, linens, artificial fibers, and so on, there are textiles and

TABLE 4–3. *United States Foreign Trade in Cotton Textiles, 1957 (by value,[a] major buyers or suppliers, and average price)*

	Value (in millions of dollars)	*Major Buyers or Suppliers (value amounts in millions of dollars)*	*Average Price per Unit (in dollars)*
		Exports	
Yarns	18.6	Philippines (4.9) Cuba (3.9)	0.941 per lb.
Sewing threads	3.8	Canada (0.8) Cuba (0.7)	1.56 per lb.
Twine, rope, cordage	2.7	Canada (0.6) Cuba (0.6)	0.719 per lb.
Cloth for embroidery and return to U.S.	3.2	Philippines (3.2)	0.327 per sq. yd.
Tire fabrics	2.6	Indonesia (1.1) South Africa (0.5)	0.500 per sq. yd.
Unbleached duck	3.4	South Africa (0.5) Norway (0.5)	0.616 per sq. yd.
Unbleached cloth	14.0	Canada (8.9) Philippines (1.5)	0.096 per sq. yd.
Finished cloth	127.5	Canada (31.7) Philippines (20.1) South Africa (13.9) Cuba (12.3)	0.329 per sq. yd.
Other fabrics	28.4	Philippines (9.9) Canada (8.6)	not available
Other	0.3		
Total	204.5		

	Value (in millions of dollars)	Major Buyers or Suppliers (value amounts in millions of dollars)	Average Price per Unit (in dollars)
		Imports	
Unbleached cloth	7.5	Japan (5.2) United Kingdom (0.7)	0.201 per sq. yd.
Bleached cloth	3.3	United Kingdom (1.9) Egypt (0.4)	0.549 per sq. yd.
Printed, dyed, or colored cloth (mostly ginghams)	24.4	Japan (12.7) Belgium (3.2) United Kingdom (2.2)	0.308 per sq. yd.
Upholstery cloth	2.9	Italy (2.2) Belgium (0.4)	not available
Velveteens	3.6	Japan (2.3) Italy (1.3)	0.851 per sq. yd.
Table damask	5.5	Japan (3.9) United Kingdom (0.6)	1.292 per lb.
Other	5.8		
Total	53.0		

[a]Major items of more than $2.5 million.

Sources: United States Department of Commerce, Bureau of the Census, *United States Exports of Domestic and Foreign Merchandise, Commodity by Country of Destination, Calendar Year 1957,* pt. I, Report No. FT 410 (Washington, D.C., G.P.O., April 1958), 111–24; and *United States Imports of Merchandise for Consumption, Commodity by Country of Origin, Calendar Year, 1957,* Report No. FT 110 (Washington, D.C., G.P.O., June 1958), 51–53.

textiles. Cheap and efficient labor provides Japan with a comparative advantage over the United States in velveteens and ginghams. But high-grade finished yarns and fine cloths —shirtings, for example—come to the United States from Britain, over a tariff wall, and threads and hand-work cottons from France. Even the United States is an exporter of some grades: industrial gauze, such as that used to shield tobacco fields against the sun during the growing season, and high-quality printcloths, exported to the high-income markets of Canada and the Union of South Africa. The industrial gauze is cheap, with a comparative advantage based on decreasing costs and long runs of machinery. But when even such a homogeneous commodity as cotton textiles is broken down into various components of quality, it appears that labor costs affect only a portion of the total, though an important one, and that comparative advantage may be based on other factors. The overall position of United States trade in cotton textiles is shown in Table 4–3.

A further important modification to the law of comparative advantage based on abundant labor is that exports can be developed only in those products for which there is a significant home market. It is not sufficient that a commodity be labor-intensive and that the country have cheap labor. For manufactured goods, or for all goods except those produced by foreign enterprises, production typically starts by providing for the domestic market and then expands to foreign outlets. Wiring radios is labor-intensive (or was before the development of printed circuits), and India is a country with teeming masses of labor. But radio exports emanate from the United States, Germany, and Britain, which have the large domestic markets to support the scale of the industry needed for exports. In a thesis for the Stockholm School of Economics, Burenstam Linder has pointed out that countries typically export goods that fit into the standard of living attained by broad numbers of their own population.[6] Japan does not export high-grade textiles because it does not consume them in quantity. The United States furnishes an opposite example. The explanation may also apply to declining export markets: Britain lost the market

6. Staffan Burenstam Linder, *An Essay on Trade and Transformation* (New York, 1961), chap. 3.

for low-grade cotton textiles—gray goods and low-count bleached cloths—primarily because of foreign competition but partly because its standard of living had risen to the point where these were unimportant items of consumption and domestic demand shifted to higher qualities. Similarly, as the American standard rose, the upgrading of the American automobile—with its large size and numerous automatic devices—brought it above the standard of countries which had previously bought United States cars, and helped to destroy its export market.

The total story has more ramifications, as will appear in part when we come to technology in Chapter 6. But strong links between the quality of exports and the requirements of the domestic market help to explain the decline of United States automobile exports from 75 per cent of the world market in 1929 to less than 5 per cent in 1959. It is an interesting game, but a difficult one, to think of manufactured products with a broad export market but only a limited domestic base. Swiss watches may be one, though that labor-intensive industry (as it used to be until recently) developed in a rich country, not one with only a moderately dense population, and flourished in World War I when both combatant neighbors had a need for the product and little available skilled labor to spare for its production. And Japanese Christmas-tree decorations may be another; but there are not many.

Another aspect of the question is quality. Great difficulty is found in marketing labor-intensive handicraft products in foreign countries because the development of broad markets requires a standardized product on which middleman and consumer can depend. This is true of both resource products and manufactures. Turkish wheat entering world markets in the late 1940s and early 1950s suffered from lack of standardization and grading, and, in some cases, allegedly, from the frequent incidence of mice and rocks among the grain. In the initial stages of its development during the American Civil War, Indian cotton was said to be filled with as much rubbish and waste as it could hold and still keep its name.[7] Denmark established itself in world butter markets after 1875 only by bringing the flavorful and interesting "peasant" butter up to the "manor" standard. Japanese foreign trade was handicapped between the world wars by a reputation for shoddy quality. Japanese foreign-trade experts developed a theory which has faded rather rapidly in the last few years, that their exports were the last to be bought in a boom and the first to be dropped in a depression—a marginal contributor, like the minority groups, "last hired, first fired," in many labor markets. Table 4–4 shows that there was something to this thesis from 1922 to 1930 and again in 1951–52. In the later 1930s and after 1953, Japanese export expansion, helped by devaluation, merely proceeded faster than world trade. Another possibility is that transport costs provide the explanation. But there is room for the "marginal supplier" theory held by the Japanese, to the extent that it is based on low quality, actual or putative. This would mean that consumers turned to Japanese goods only when other supplies were unavailable at their usual prices.

Since World War II Japan has made an impressive effort to convert its export trade from reliance on low-quality, labor-intensive commodities to those of higher technology. New exports have appeared on world markets, like locomotives in the engineering trades, and cameras and binoculars, to rival the German specialties. All these, and even the prewar exports, have been rigorously controlled in quality. Ta-

7. David S. Landes, *Bankers and Pashas* (Cambridge, Mass., Harvard University Press, 1958), pp. 71–72.

TABLE 4–4. *Changes in Japanese and World Exports Compared in Current Values*
(percentage increase or decrease over previous year)

Year	*Japan*	*World*
1922	30	+7[a]
1923	−12	+5[a]
1924	24	+11[a]
1925	27	+14[a]
1926	−11	−3
1927	−7	5
1928	25	3
1929	8	2
1930	−28	−20
1931	−21	−29
1932	22	−32
1933	31	−9
1934	23	−3
1935	18	2
1936	10	8
1937	17	23
1951	65	36
1952	−6	−4
1953	0	2
1954	28	4
1955	23	9
1956	24	11
1957	14	8
1958	1	−5

[a]Series not strictly comparable.

Sources: Japan: 1922–27, *Annuaire Statistique de France, 1951* (Paris, 1952); 1928–37, United Nations, *Statistical Yearbook 1948;* 1948–57, United Nations, *Yearbook of International Trade Statistics, 1959* (New York, 1960). World: 1921–26, worksheets for League of Nations, *Review of World Trade, 1933* (Geneva, 1934), *1939* (Geneva, 1940); 1951–58, United Nations, *Yearbook of International Trade Statistics, 1956* and *1959*. The early figures contain a large and unexplained figure for unreported trade, possibly representing smuggling of liquor into the United States during Prohibition.

ble 4–5 shows the change in the structure of Japanese manufactured exports. The result of these changes has been to alter materially the picture of Japan as a country exporting labor-intensive goods. A recent study shows, in fact, that Japanese exports are capital- rather than labor-intensive. The degree of capital intensity differs between areas, however, and exports to the United States are less capital-intensive than those sold to Asian countries.[8]

TABLE 4–5. *Evolution of the Japanese Export Structure, 1913–1958 (percentage of certain classes in total exports of manufactures)*

	1913	*1923*	*1934–36*	*1953*	*1958*
Textiles (excl. raw silk)	30	40	41	33	30
Machinery, transport equipment	2	2	7	15	22
Instruments	—	—	—	1	2
Labor-intensive manufactures[a]	11	5	n.a.[b]	7	5
Toys	1	1	1	2	2

[a]As described by Uyehara for 1913 and 1923. For 1953 and 1958 it is goods not elsewhere specified.
[b]Not available.

Sources: 1913, 1923, S. Uyehara, *The Trade and Industry of Japan* (London, King, 1926), pp. 62–64; 1934–36, G. C. Allen, *Japan's Economic Recovery* (London, Oxford University Press, 1958), appendix table 14; 1953, 1958, United Nations, *Yearbook of International Trade Statistics, 1954, 1959.*

8. Masahiro Tatemoto and Shinichi Ichimura, "Factor Proportions and Foreign Trade: The Case of Japan," *Review of Economics and Statistics, 41* (1959), 442–46. This study, using input-output methods, was undertaken after the pattern of the Leontief study of United States trade, discussed in the next chapter, which produced the paradoxical result that the United States exported labor-intensive and imported capital-intensive products. The conclusion that Japanese exports are capital-intensive is equally paradoxical and may be as unacceptable as the Leontief findings.

This general argument must be qualified, however. Whereas velveteens and ginghams, ladies' blouses and knit gloves are labor-intensive in the sense that applies readily around the world—though not all countries will have the capacity to organize production and marketing as efficiently as Japan (and Hong Kong)—cameras and binoculars, scientific instruments and electronic equipment, and so on (including products of diamond cutting in Belgium and gold-leaf rolling in pre-Hitler Germany) are labor-intensive only in terms of highly trained and specialized skills, and exports of such products cannot be predicted from high labor–land or labor–capital ratios.

UNDERDEVELOPED, LABOR-INTENSIVE ECONOMIES

A country with abundant labor and available resources in land may be led, in the view of some writers, to "overexporting."[9] The reasoning is as follows: with surplus labor available at very low wage rates, it pays plantation owners to push exports of such products as sugar, rubber, coffee, tea, bananas, even though the demand may be relatively inelastic. Until productivity can be raised in the domestic food sector of the economy, or—more difficult—in expanded industry, thus raising the return in alternative employments and hence wages, any increase in productivity in the export sector will accrue to the consumer abroad or to the landowner at home (who may well be a foreigner), with little benefit to domestic labor. It is only when labor productivity has been raised in all fields, disguised unemployment (i.e. labor producing little or nothing) in agriculture removed, and labor appropriately allocated among the export, domestic,

9. Lewis, *Theory of Economic Growth,* p. 281.

and import-competing sectors that a country can be said to be exporting in the proper proportions.

This view was first put forward from a different perspective by a Rumanian economist, Mihail Manoilescu, who used it as an argument for protection. He regarded wages in industry as artificially high, which limited employment in import-competing lines, raised costs and prices, and unduly encouraged imports. Tariffs, in his judgment, were needed to offset, from a social point of view, the inappropriate market encouragement to imports given by the too high level of wages in industry and the redundant pent-up labor in agriculture.[10]

It is true that if factor markets are imperfect, the free-trade solution will not give a welfare maximum. (If they are perfect, what's more, the welfare maximum exists only for the given distribution of income.) If other factor markets function effectively, and labor alone suffers from poor allocation, with too little labor at too high a price in industry, and too much at too low in agriculture, "overexporting" and "overimporting" may take place, and require correction through tariffs or export taxes. The ideal policy is to remove the distortion in factor market pricing. A tariff on imports or an export tax is only a second-best policy.

Other factors may be badly allocated too, however, with overinvestment in industry, for example, and underinvestment in agriculture. Before free trade is abandoned to correct for alleged disguised unemployment in agriculture, the allocation of all factors should be examined. Moreover, it may be possible in some cases to correct the disguised unemployment within the agricultural sector, shifting from land-intensive to labor-intensive crops—that is, from sugar to tobac-

10. Mihail Manoilescu, *The Theory of Protection and International Trade* (London, 1931).

co in Cuba for example, or from grains and so-called technical crops (oilseeds and fibers) to labor-intensive fruit and vegetables in Bulgaria.[11] If this can be done, it may be possible to increase productive employment and exports at the same time.

DUAL ECONOMIES

Imperfections of factor markets that inhibit the achievement of a trade-welfare optimum are of course abundant in underdeveloped countries. One of the most usual, called a dual economy, arises from the division of the domestic economy, and sometimes also the foreign-trade sector, into two parts: one combining native land, native labor, and virtually no capital; the other involving native land, foreign capital and management, and limited numbers of native workers. Foreign entrepreneurship typically adheres to capital-intensive factor proportions, despite the availability of abundant labor, because of habit in clinging to a known technology, the absence of alternative factor combinations (as in drilling and transporting oil), the insistence of local authorities on modern techniques, or for other reasons. The result is dual economy—a modern sector which, Singer has suggested, really represents an enclave abroad belonging to the capital-investing country,[12] and the indigenous sector. Sometimes

11. Charles A. Cooper, "Agriculture, Labor Supply and Foreign Trade in Bulgaria, 1925–1960" (doctoral dissertation, Massachusetts Institute of Technology, 1960); and appendix to Carl Major Wright, *Economic Adaptation to a Changing World Market* (Copenhagen, Munksgaard, 1939). Cooper points out that after World War II the Soviet Union provided the demand for labor-intensive exports which had come from Schactian Germany in the late 1930s.

12. Hans W. Singer, "The Distribution of Gains between Investing and Borrowing Countries," *American Economic Review, Papers and Proceedings, 40* (1950), 473.

exports are produced only by the foreign sector—Middle East oil, for example, Rhodesian copper, and African diamonds and gold. Sometimes the same commodities are produced side by side in the two sectors, as in Central American bananas, Southeast Asian rubber, Ceylon and Indian tea. How necessary the foreign skill is to the domestic producers, especially if they can appropriate the foreign capital, will vary from case to case, as was learned after the confiscations of the Anglo-Iranian oil refinery at Abadan, in one case, and of the Suez Canal, in another. But the existence of a dual economy creates tensions that may impede development.

Dutch writers on Indonesia explain dual economies in terms of differing social organizations: on the one hand, there are Western societies, with unlimited wants, a money economy, and corporate organization; on the other, the Eastern peoples, whose needs are social rather than economic, who respond to higher wages by offering less work rather than more (the so-called "backward-bending supply curve for labor") and who have no idea of seeking profit as a regular basis of income, as opposed to the casual, strike-it-rich approach.[13] In Venezuela the existence of the oil companies with their high wages for a limited number of local employees may stimulate the economy through government investment of taxes collected from the companies, but it may also be inhibiting, insofar as it encourages the potential local entrepreneur to stand in line for a job with the company, rather than to work, save, and build a business in other activities.

It is evidently difficult to use the price system as an indication of the appropriate allocation of resources, and especially

13. J. H. Boeke, *Economics and Economic Policy of Dual Societies as Exemplified by Indonesia* (New York, Institute of Pacific Relations, 1953).

of labor, in foreign trade when the price system works either badly or not at all. We shall recur to this platitude later. The Heckscher-Ohlin theorem nonetheless retains value as a rough guide to economic possibilities. A labor-intensive, land-poor country need not start off in foreign trade through labor-intensive exports—but Japan did. And if the Heckscher-Ohlin theorem does not apply in detail, it does not follow that it can be ignored, with every underdeveloped country setting out to acquire hot and cold integrated steel rolling mills.

5 CAPITAL

CAPITAL, SCALE, AND TECHNOLOGY

Discussion of capital abundance and capital scarcity as a cause of international trade is fraught with difficulty. Possibly for this reason it is generally avoided.[1] Taussig and Viner, who were aware of the law of variable proportions, tried to dismiss capital on the ground of unimportance in the final outcome. Viner claimed that capital–labor ratios are just about the same in every industry, and that even when they differ, the cost of capital, in terms of interest, tends to be small compared with the cost of labor.[2]

The difficulties are factual, as will be seen shortly. But

1. MacDougall, "British and American Exports."
2. Jacob Viner, *Studies in the Theory of International Trade* (New York, 1937), pp. 510 ff.

they are also conceptual. In Chapter 3 we mentioned the difficulty of distinguishing land from capital. There are also problems of separating it from the scale of enterprises, from technical change, and even from labor, with varying degrees of education and accumulated skill. Again, is capital a fungible mass of financial means of investment, available for this or that undertaking, or does it consist of specific structures, equipment, and inventories which are useful only for limited purposes? How is capital measured in its contribution to output—by the initial amount needed, or by the amount used up each year? The two measures will differ widely for equal values of capital with very different lengths of life.

Capital theory abounds in conundrums of this sort, which it is no part of the task of this monograph to resolve. Our position may be limited to stating that while there are difficulties in distinguishing capital from other factors, in deciding whether to deal with it *ex ante* or *ex post,* and in its measurement, it is probably dangerous to ignore it as a cause of trade.

It may be useful, however, to spend a moment on the relations between capital, on the one hand, and scale and technology, on the other. Just before World War I orthodox economics, represented at the time by the youthful John Maynard (later Lord) Keynes, held that primary production and manufacturing were subject to different laws: the former to diminishing returns (the more labor and capital were applied to land, the lower their marginal product would be), the latter to increasing returns (the greater the output, the lower the cost per unit until some low-cost point was reached, after which cost per unit rose again). From this contrast Keynes drew the conclusion, which is contrary to one held widely today, that the long-run terms of trade between primary products and manufactures would favor the former over the latter.[3]

Primary production is identified with land, but manufacturing is, of course, not necessarily capital-intensive. Adam Smith's classic example of increasing returns to scale in pinmaking describes a labor-intensive process.[4] But, while high capital intensity and large-scale enterprise are not identical, large-scale enterprises typically use capital abundantly, and very capital-intensive projects are generally large in scale. The issue turns partly on how capital intensity is defined, whether exclusively in terms of the capital–labor ratio, or in terms of the absolute amount of capital invested as well. For the moment we exclude the small-scale enterprise with a high capital–labor ratio—say $50,000 worth of two-hundred-year-old olive trees, farmed by one man on one acre of land.

Identification of decreasing returns with land-intensive processes and increasing returns with capital-intensive may be correct. But it is clearly a mistake, in retrospect, to link decreasing returns to primary production and increasing returns to manufacturing. As Chapter 3 noted,[5] primary production is often exploited in capital-intensive ways, with land and capital as complements instead of substitutes. Petroleum production, aluminum refining, open-cast and deep-shaft mining are simultaneously land- and capital-intensive. They are also economical only on a substantial scale.

Mass production involves more than capital. It also requires a change in technology. World War I saw the intro-

3. Note on the "Return of Estimated Value of Foreign Trade of the United Kingdom at Prices of 1900," *Economic Journal*, 22 (1912), 631.

4. Adam Smith, *An Inquiry into the Nature and Causes of the Wealth of Nations*, bk. I chap. 1.

5. See p. 42.

duction of mass production by the United States; World War II, mass precision—the achievement of close tolerances by machine rather than hand-controlled methods. It is sometimes added that the next task of technology is to achieve a new spectrum of materials, designed or compounded for specific uses, with special capacities to resist or conduct heat, cold, electrical charges, and so on. But this matter can wait until Chapter 6. Here we observe only that technical change may be the result of inspiration—an intensive experience of a limited sort of labor—but that change may stem from organized research, which in turn can be regarded as capital.

Money capital is a passive rather than an active source of trade, and this may explain its neglect by the classical economists. With iron ore, or a new way to weave cotton textiles, there is no problem of choosing an industry to enter, provided one can obtain the capital. But the possession of capital without access to unexploited resources or new technology points to no clear outcome. In the period between the development of textiles and railroads up to the 1870s and the electrical, mechanical, and chemical revolution at the end of the nineteenth century, British and French capital went abroad to finance new railroad construction—for lack of obvious investment opportunities at home.

But it is nonetheless true that with abundant capital a country ultimately acquires a comparative advantage in capital-intensive products. The classical example is probably the chemical industry in the United States. Prior to World War I, Germany was the world leader in chemicals, largely because of technical superiority. Its comparative advantage rested on the respect in which scientists were held, which enabled the country to produce Ph.D.'s in chemistry who were numerous and therefore cheap. But chemical processes are capital-intensive. After the war the United States was a country with relatively abundant capital. The confiscation of German patents by the Alien Property Custodian provided the technology. Scale was achieved through the imposition of customs duties, on the ground of national defense. And the industry took hold. Here was justification of the infant-industry argument for a tariff. The proof: the industry ultimately became an exporter in world markets. This outcome was due, of course, to technological advances in the United States, based on capital investment in organized research.

There are chemical lines in which the United States retains a comparative disadvantage. The industry reacts strongly against proposals for customs simplification—the regularization of valuation procedures with no change in effective rates of duty—because it would reveal how many hundred per cent is the rate of protection in some standard-process bulk products. But the industry is a net exporter and provides proof that a country with abundant capital and the requisite technology can acquire a comparative advantage in capital-intensive products. This is a very weak statement, however. The capital is a necessary condition, but not a sufficient one.

THE LEONTIEF PARADOX

The foregoing asserts or strongly implies that the United States is a capital-intensive economy. This common belief was challenged a few years ago by Wassily Leontief. In the course of his work on the structure of the United States economy, using input-output tables, Leontief came to the conclusion, on the basis of the 1947 foreign trade returns, that the United States had a comparative advantage in labor-intensive commodities, and a disadvantage in capital-intensive ones.[6] The original finding created a furor in international trade theory which is only just beginning to die down. It led, in fact, to a fairly fundamental revision of the Heckscher-Ohlin theorem.

Leontief's technique was to compare the capital–labor ratios for new capacity in United States export and import-competing industries. Capital was measured by the amount of new capital needed to build capacity to produce a million dollars' worth of additional product a year. This is the total capital-to-output ratio, not the ratio of capital consumed; and the ratio at the margin, not on the average. (These are not criticisms, but indications of the choices made.) Labor intensity was measured in man-days needed to produce a million dollars of incremental output. The results of the initial tabulation showed that the capital–labor ratio in import-competing goods at $18,200 was higher than the $14,000 figure for exports.

In the light of the accepted view that American exports are capital-intensive, and imports labor-intensive, this finding is a paradox. Leontief attempts to explain the paradox by the suggestion that American labor is three times as productive as labor elsewhere—even apart from the productivity of its associated capital—and that therefore one should multiply the American labor supply by three. This explanation accords with the theoretical model. It could rest, if true, on the higher average education of American workers, on their greater interest in output or in income, or on better organization.

6. W. W. Leontief, "Domestic Production and Foreign Trade: The American Capital Position Re-examined," *Proceedings* of the American Philosophical Society, *97* (1953), 332–49. The paper is reproduced in a source more accessible to economists in *Economia Internazionale, 7* (1954), 9–38.

These findings were not readily accepted. One criticism was that the 1947 trade returns were not typical. That year saw a huge export surplus financed by foreign loans: exports were double imports in value, and the normal complement of manufactured imports from Europe, still recovering from the war, was lacking. Taking this criticism into account, Leontief redid the calculations, using 1951 trade. He also recomputed 1947 trade on the basis of a more detailed input-output table. Each recalculation reduced the disparity between capital–output ratios, but left import-competing industry slightly ahead of export industry. (See Table 5–1.)

TABLE 5–1. *Capital–Labor Ratios in United States Export and Import-Competing Industries, 1947 and 1951, as Calculated by Leontief*

	Capital–Labor Ratios (in dollars per man-year)		*Import Ratio / Export Ratio*
	Exports	*Import-Replacements*	
1947 original	14,010	18,180	1.30
1947 revised	11,622	13,658	1.18
1951	12,977	13,726	1.06

Source: 1947 original, Leontief, table 2. Others: W. W. Leontief, "Factor Proportions and the Structure of American Foreign Trade: Further Theoretical and Empirical Analysis," *Review of Economics and Statistics, 38* (1956), 397–98, table 1.

There was objection to limiting the analysis to two factors, particularly as resources were of importance in both exports and imports, and Leontief's coefficients seemed to bespeak a confusion between land and capital. (Almost the highest capital coefficient—4.7—was for agriculture and fisheries, compared with figures of 2.0 to 3.0 in heavy industry such as steel, blast furnaces, and automobile manufacture.) Jaroslav Vanek has shown that much of the capital in imports is complementary to resources.[7] Leontief himself is engaged in modifying his results to take natural resources explicitly into account, but the results are not available as this is written.

The major objection to the paradox, however, is that it rests on an invalid part of the Heckscher-Ohlin theorem —that commodities are typically produced within narrowly variable factor proportions. In an early comment on the first article, Ellsworth was reaching for this objection when he said that Leontief should have compared the capital–labor ratio in United States exports with the capital–labor ratio *abroad* in United States imports.[8] This would have enabled Leontief to take into account the capital–labor ratios in a number of articles like coffee, tea, bananas, and tin, which are not produced at all in the United States. But this does not meet the point. Leontief's technique was appropriate as a test of the Heckscher-Ohlin theorem, which assumes that production techniques are the same the world over and that they allow little room for factor substitution. What he proves is not that the United States is capital-scarce and labor-abundant, but that the Heckscher-Ohlin theorem is wrong.

Production functions and factors have to be defined in terms of one another. If these are broadly defined, so that all countries have the same production functions and but two factors, the Heckscher-Ohlin theorem fails on the requirement that the same good must always be labor-intensive or capital-intensive, whatever the relative factor prices (or

7. "The Natural Resource Content of Foreign Trade, 1870–1955, and the Relative Abundance of Natural Resources in the United States," *Review of Economics and Statistics, 41* (1959), 146–53.

8. P. T. Ellsworth, "The Structure of American Foreign Trade: A New View Examined," *Review of Economics and Statistics, 36* (1954), 279–85.

that factor endowments between countries will not differ so much as to bring commodities into the range where production methods will differ). If Indonesia and the United States produce rubber on the same production function, but rubber is labor-intensive in Indonesia and capital-intensive in the United States, factor proportions cannot be used to forecast the nature of trade, and the Heckscher-Ohlin theorem cannot apply. It is evidently absurd to regard the United States as capital-scarce if capital is so abundant that it is used freely to substitute for labor; or Indonesia as capital-abundant if it can export a product which the United States produces capital-intensively, by substituting labor for capital. When goods change their factor intensities from country to country, depending on factor endowments and factor prices, the Heckscher-Ohlin theorem falls to the ground.

Or factors and production functions can be defined narrowly, with many factors, and even a difference between natural and synthetic rubber. In this case the Heckscher-Ohlin theorem fails because not every country has the same set of factors and can use the same production functions, as required by the theorem.

It was indicated in an earlier chapter that cotton has changed from a labor- and land-intensive commodity to a capital-intensive one.[9] The same is true of wheat, and of chickens, eggs, and many other farm products. United States exports of agricultural products fell drastically after World War I, as labor became scarcer and agricultural products were still being produced by relatively labor-intensive methods. But with the agricultural revolution in the late 1930s, and especially during World War II, the substitution of capital for labor and land has enabled the United States to win

9. See p. 50.

back its old comparative advantage in a number of these commodities. The position cannot be clearly demonstrated because of the distortion introduced by the policies of Congress and the Department of Agriculture, which first raise prices and then subsidize exports. Most expert opinion, however, is of the view that in a free market the United States would have a comparative advantage in the production and export of wheat, on the grounds of its capital-abundance and the capital-intensive methods of modern production.

THE HECKSCHER-OHLIN THEOREM AND ECONOMIC HISTORY

The Leontief paradox thus proves not that the United States factor proportions are otherwise than what is conventionally thought, but that the basic assumption of relatively fixed proportions of factor inputs in different commodities, fundamental to the Heckscher-Ohlin theorem, is invalid. The increasing range of substitutability of factors is new. The Heckscher-Ohlin theorem, combined with a mild form of economic interpretation of politics, remains a useful guide to an understanding of past commercial policy.

Until 1846 Britain used tariffs to protect its landowners, who had dominant political power. By maintaining the price of wheat and of farm rentals, it sustained the relative return to the scarce but politically powerful factor. But political centers of gravity shift. With the Reform Bill of 1832, which reduced the number of rotten boroughs and provided for more popular representation in the House of Commons, the rising industrial and commercial classes challenged the political domination of the landed gentry. The economic interest of the former was served not by tariffs but by free trade, increased exports of Lancashire textiles, and increased imports of food to hold down the cost of living and the level of wages. Hence the repeal of the Corn Laws and the subsequent movement to free trade which culminated in the Anglo-French Treaty of Commerce of 1860.

A similar analysis can be worked out for the tariff history of the United States, in terms of the early free-trade interests of the land-intensive South, as opposed to the protectionism of the scarce factor, capital, with its major location in the North and Middle West. Changes in factor endowments, in the technology of production, and in the location of industry have altered the applicability of the original analysis: as a producer of labor-intensive textiles, the South today is no longer as free-trade minded as it was, though cultural lag results in some persistence of the traditional view. The Reciprocal Trade Agreements Act, setting in train a reduction of United States tariffs, was a delayed response to the interest of the Middle West in mass production and the export of its output. Detroit became, for a time, the Manchester of the United States. Capital remained politically dominant, but it turned from import-competing, small-scale production to the decreasing-cost industries which were able to sell abroad. And finally the protectionist attitude of the North began to weaken, as textiles and fisheries lost in importance to electronics, and it became necessary to buy cheap fuel oil from abroad at a price below that at which Texas and Louisiana would like to hold it.

THE STRUCTURE OF TRADE AND FACTOR PROPORTIONS

While land may be taken as fixed (if we disregard discovery and depletion), and labor changes but slowly from one generation to another (in the absence of migration), capital can be accumulated rapidly. Not only is capital mobile internationally, to a greater extent than labor, but it can be accumulated domestically, by productive countries, in a short period of time. In periods of recovery after both world wars, observers have been astonished at how quickly capital can be restored after apparent widespread destruction. The fact is that capital is a relatively small multiple of national income —between twice and three times. If net capital formation is maintained at 25 per cent a year—a high but not impossible figure—the destruction and accumulated depreciation of five years of war, which can hardly amount to 50 per cent of the capital stock, or one year's income at a capital–output ratio of 2:1, can be made up in four years.

Immediately after World War II, the drastic change in the economic condition of Western Germany seemed to call for a new structure of trade. Land had been lost to the Soviet Union and to Poland and in the splitting of zones of occupation into the three western and one eastern. The labor supply rose because of the return of the Volksdeutsche from abroad and the flood of refugees from the East. Capital destruction was far-reaching. With an entirely new set of factor proportions—sharp increases in the labor–land and labor–capital ratios—a new foreign trade structure seemed called for, one that would emphasize labor-intensive exports and land- and capital-intensive imports.

Table 5–2, however, shows that there was little change in the structure of German trade between 1936 and the postwar period, such as might have been expected from a far-reaching change in factor proportions. Moreover exports of finished goods have continued to emphasize the products of heavy industry—machinery, machine tools, chemicals, electrical equipment. And raw materials dominate imports, but are supplemented by imports of consumers' goods, not exports.

TABLE 5–2. *The Structure of German Foreign Trade, 1936, 1954, 1955 (percentage breakdown by broad commodity classes)*

	Exports			*Imports*		
	1936 (Germany)	*1954*	*1955 (West Germany and West Berlin)*	*1936 (Germany)*	*1954*	*1955 (West Germany and West Berlin)*
Foodstuffs	2	3	2	36	37	37
Industrial products						
Raw materials	9	8	8	37	33	29
Semifinished goods	10	15	13	18	15	18
Finished goods	80	75	77	9	16	17
Subtotal	98	97	98	64	63	63
Total	100	100	100	100	100	100

Source: Statistiches Bundesamt, *Wirtschaftskunde der Bundesrepublik Deutschlands* (Stuttgart and Cologne, 1955), p. 522.

Instead of adapting its foreign trade to its factor proportions, Germany altered the proportions to the trade. United States relief assistance and Marshall Plan aid provided the start, but intensive saving over an extended period made up the absolute loss of capital, and provided new capital on a high capital–labor ratio for the added labor. If any change occurred in response to the changed factor proportions, it was in the treatment of certain functions within the plant, such as materials handling, though not in direct production processes. Even this concession to the changed conditions cannot be demonstrated for lack of facts. But there was little adaptation of the trade structure.

A similar apparent disregard of factor proportions in favor of heavy industry, and especially chemicals and steel, has been followed in Dutch postwar economic planning. The return of migrants from the colonies, the loss of colonial outlets for migration, and a high birth rate should have led, in economic theory, to a change in the foreign-trade structure in favor of labor-intensive exports and land-cum-capital-intensive imports. But this consideration was virtually ignored. Capital accumulation proceeded, and even the creation of new land (capital?) through the damming of the Zuider Zee and the building of new polders through pumping, filling, and desalination. Dutch agriculture continues to be highly labor-intensive and export-oriented, with its tulip bulbs, vegetables, and cheeses. But investment in chemicals, oil refining, and steel have been undertaken on a large scale, and only partly with foreign capital.

Jean Weiller, the French economist, has tried to introduce into international trade theory a new term which would explain this phenomenon. Countries, he states, have a preference for certain structures.[10] To the general equilibrium theorist this reasoning has little appeal, since the structure is expected to adapt to the factor endowments and technological possibilities existing in the country, relative to the rest of the world. Policy decisions can interfere with this theoretical equilibrium structure, but, to be sure, so can the existence of past capital in given industries (which may reduce the capital requirements at the margin for entering those industries); and so may past habits of thought. Prestige in Germany has always gone to those entrepreneurs who specialize in armaments and heavy industry (including exports), according to William Parker.[11] And to the extent of

10. Jean Weiller and Jacques Duvaux, *Economie française, échanges extérieurs, et structures internationales,* Cahiers de l'Institut de Science Economique Appliquée, sér. P, no. 1 (1957).

11. "Entrepreneurial Opportunities and Response in the German Economy," *Explorations in Entrepreneurial History,* 7 (1954), 26–36.

these two factors, there may be something to the notion of a preference for a given structure. There is no wiping the slate clean and starting again. Inertia or hysteresis helps to shape the present in terms of the past.

TRADE OR CAPITAL MOVEMENTS

Capital is par excellence the internationally mobile factor, and, as mentioned, capital movements can substitute for trade in capital-intensive goods.[12] Whether it is goods or capital that moves in any particular case is an open question; when there is no barrier to the movement of either, the answer is indeterminate. But typically there will be some force which tips the scales—either tariffs, which inhibit the movement of goods and thereby stimulate the movement of the factor, or the existence of complementary factors in greater abundance and cheaper in one location than in the other. Capital may feel that it belongs in one country and is on an alien basis in another. In any particular instance, there will be a series of influences moving in each direction which require a careful weighing. But if capital could produce by itself alone, it would make no difference whether there were trade in capital-intensive goods or capital movements.

As it is, the mobility of capital means that countries which are short of capital can rely on foreign capital. This will typically occur only when the large amounts of capital are needed in conjunction with specialized other resources—the dam sites on the Volta River in Ghana or at the Kariba Gorge in Rhodesia. When the mountain cannot be brought to Mohammed, Mohammed does the traveling.

In still other cases, however, the question will be entirely

12. Mundell, "International Trade and Factor Mobility."

open. Should du Pont export nylon to France, or export capital to build a plant there for local output? The answer may turn on consideration of location economics—the supply- or market-oriented characteristics of the product; tariff or capital-import or export policies of the countries concerned; or even such questions as patent laws, which rarely enter economic analysis but which are nonetheless not insignificant. But we cannot go far in this question on a theoretical basis. What happens will depend on the facts of the individual case.

6 TECHNOLOGY

Neoclassical economics assumed a "given state of the arts"—that is, a fixed and unchanging technology, existing everywhere in the world and accessible to every trading nation. With a given technology, factors could be uniquely defined. Comparative advantage could be expressed in terms of factor endowments.

A given state of the arts simplified the analysis, and, in a world where technology changes only slowly, the assumption may be appropriate. But in our world it is no longer so. Changes in technology occur, initially, in a limited area, and take time to spread to all countries. They may be systematic in their origin. Technological change will affect comparative advantage, transitionally in any event, and possibly in the long run. Today's discussion of international trade must treat technical change and its diffusion.

Technology

INVENTION AND INNOVATION

Schumpeter analyzed the process of technical change in terms of two processes: invention and innovation. Invention was the creative act of insight, involving a new combination of matter, a discontinuity, and a break with the past, making possible the creation of a new product or the devising of a new technique to produce an existing good more cheaply. Innovation was the act of making the new product or process economically viable. Schumpeter believed that these acts were separate in character, requiring different types of personality and temperament. Invention was the task of the engineer-tinkerer or scientist, innovation the work of the entrepreneur-businessman.[1]

Inventions have come in waves, bunched in time and usually in space. The same inventive idea may occur more or less simultaneously to two or more men in one or more countries. There is great difficulty in recognizing where credit for the invention of a complex mechanism belongs. Some inventions occur well before the world is ready to receive them: a Polish inventor who conceived machinery for weaving cloth in the twelfth century was hanged for his threat to the world about him. Other inventions seem to be adroitly suited to current needs—the offsprings of that well-known parent, Necessity.

If invention and innovation occurred in random fashion throughout the world, now here, now there, the disturbance of any one would be the same, but the effects would not be so great because they would not be cumulative. It is an important question, therefore, whether invention and, more

1. J. A. Schumpeter, *Business Cycles* (New York and London, 1939), *1*, 84 ff.

significantly, innovation are biased in their incidence and in their impact on trade. Of greatest importance for long-term trends may be change in the systematic bias of technology—the emergence of new technological leaders and the subsiding of old.

The Industrial Revolution occurred in Britain, spread to the European continent, then to the United States. In the early stages there was a tendency for inventions to occur widely but to be applied most quickly in Britain. The French had a hand in the development of steam power, but the British were years ahead in applying it. The Jacquard loom crossed the Channel for its full application to textiles. And so on. During this period, to about 1860, Britain clearly outshone the world in innovation, though it had no monopoly on invention.

After 1860, German and United States innovative capacity began to be more noticeable, and British to recede. The Thomas process, developed in England, was used mainly in German and later French Lorraine. As industry became more complex, invention passed from the shop of the gifted amateur to the scientific laboratory, and favored the Continent, with its tradition of scientific education, over Britain, which had neglected science in favor of the classics. Even on the Continent there were differences from country to country. Parker has observed that in the iron and steel industries, French inventions, based on scientific rationalism, were applicable in many countries, whereas German inventions were directed to the solution of peculiarly narrow practical problems facing German industry.[2] As United States growth proceeded, its innovative capacity waxed, aided by America's

2. W. N. Parker, "Comment" on C. P. Kindleberger, "International Trade and Investment, and Resource Use," in J. J. Spengler, ed., *Natural Resources and Economic Growth* (Washington, D.C., 1961), pp. 187–90.

physical remoteness from World War I and its task as an armory. Inventions might be European in origin, whether of the automobile or radio, or the fundamental discoveries of the atom which preceded the construction of the bomb. America—the home of Bell, Morse, and Edison—was not lacking in inventors, but the deeper impression on the world economy was made by the McCormicks, Firestones, and Fords.

Innovation may then have been biased, i.e. distributed unevenly, nationally, in character and amount. Bias in invention has been less marked, though limited to developed countries. The second half of the twentieth century may see a growth of bias in invention, as the creative process changes from the brilliant flash of insight into the systematic canvas of possibilities.[3] Not all room for inspiration has been eliminated. But the locus of invention may depend more on which country has the biggest national defense budget, from which inventions emerge as a by-product, or the largest (or best?) system of technical education.

What is the impact on trade if invention and innovation are biased? Something depends on whether they occur in new goods, or in cheapening the cost of familiar ones. A new good—and in this we exclude a close substitute for an existing one which may replace an import—is likely to expand exports to the extent that other countries are unable initially to produce it but want to consume it. This is "protrade bias." New ways of making old goods can either expand trade (protrade bias) or, as in the case of synthetic substitutes for primary product imports, reduce it (antitrade bias). The

3. John Jewkes, David Sawers, and Richard Stillerman, *The Sources of Invention* (London, Macmillan, 1958), are deeply skeptical of all generalizations of this sort.

distinction cannot be pushed very far. Some innovations may so reduce the cost of an import that the country becomes able to sell it abroad successfully. It is then both antitrade and protrade biased.

John Hicks has argued that there has been a fundamental difference between British and United States innovations. The former in the eighteenth and nineteenth centuries were, in his view, protrade biased, introducing cheaper articles into foreign trade (especially cotton cloth) and new goods (railroad equipment, steel, ships). The United States with its nylon for silk, Buna-S for rubber (a German invention), synthetic nitrates (also German in origin), plastics, and so on has been readier to innovate with an antitrade bias. In Hicks' view, this difference helped to explain why the United States, up to the early 1950s, gave rise to a dollar shortage when it was the leading country in international trade, when the United Kingdom had not produced a persistent shortage of sterling.[4]

The evidence for this difference in bias has been examined by MacDougall, and held to be unconvincing.[5] In fact, there is authority to the contrary—that the persistent disequilibrium in the United States balance of payments, when it produced a surplus, or a shortage of dollars before 1958—was the result of innovation in new goods which the rest of the world found irresistible. Sir Geoffrey Crowther is responsible for perhaps the most extreme statement of this point of view:[6] "There are so many American goods that the world

4. John R. Hicks, "An Inaugural Lecture," *Oxford Economic Papers*, n.s., 5 (1953), 117–35.

5. G. D. A. MacDougall, *The World Dollar Problem* (London, 1957), especially appendix VIc, pp. 512–19.

6. Sir Geoffrey Crowther, *Balances and Imbalances of Payments* (Boston, Harvard University School of Business Administration, 1957), p. 51.

wants, whatever they cost." The same thought is central to the analysis of other writers.[7]

There may then be bias from time to time in the locus of innovations, but it is unlikely that they tend, on balance, to contract trade more than they expand it. Articles do disappear from trade: Peruvian guano, Chilean nitrates, Japanese silk, Chinese hog bristles and tung oil (with political assistance). Natural edible and inedible fats and oils face difficulty from detergents, and there is the major threat of synthetic coffee. But technical change has worked mainly to expand trade. It is not necessary to go back to the beginnings of the Industrial Revolution to show this, or to the successive entry into trade of textiles, galvanized iron, electrical equipment, chemicals, durable consumers' goods, and machine tools. Lamartine Yates has produced a table (6–1) showing the

TABLE 6–1. *The Structure of World Exports, 1913 and 1953 (percentage breakdown by broad commodity classes)*

Class	*1913*	*1953*
Foodstuffs	29	23
Agricultural raw materials	21	14
Minerals	13	20
Manufactures	37	43

Source: P. Lamartine Yates, *Forty Years of Foreign Trade,* appendix table A–17.

broad changes in the composition of world trade between 1913 and 1953, with an enormous rise of minerals (largely petroleum, iron, and steel) and of manufactures. The first of the declining groups—agricultural raw materials—has shrunk absolutely as a consequence of the decline of silk,

7. Erik Hoffmeyer, *Dollar Shortage and the Structure of U.S. Foreign Trade* (Copenhagen, 1958).

but foodstuffs have expanded absolutely. The increase in trade in manufactures has been so far-reaching, and the changes in the composition of trade in this area so drastic, that many commentators object to all statements that deal with the volume or average price of trade over long periods of time on the ground that no comparison is possible between such disparate sets of goods.[8]

IMITATION IN CONSUMPTION

New goods in international trade raise the question of the "demonstration effect," touched upon in Chapter 3.[9] The attempt to buy such goods may give rise to balance-of-payments difficulties, if the purchases are financed by drawing down cash balances or expanding credit, rather than by the diversion of expenditure from other imports, from exports which free them for sale abroad, or from domestic goods, which free resources for export expansion or import replacement. This question is important, though it does not concern us here. The demonstration effect may also work in the opposite direction, spreading an appetite for income, inducing peoples who previously were content with a given standard of living to work harder to earn the new goods.

Goods bought because of demonstration effect may have a symbolic rather than a physical importance for the society, although perhaps all wants above a low minimum are socially determined. The three most popular articles of Western consumption in the East are said to be the wrist watch, which stands for time in a traditional society where time has stood still; the fountain pen, symbolizing literacy; and the bicycle, representing mobility. But fads in consumption apply internationally in developed countries as well: Paris

8. J. Viner, *International Trade and Economic Development* (Glencoe, Ill., 1952), pp. 143–44.

9. See p. 27.

gowns, British suits, Italian hats, European small cars, Scotch whisky—the list could be multiplied endlessly.

IMITATION IN PRODUCTION

But demonstration effect is not confined to consumption, which includes the purchase of producers' goods where no additional work is done and no less labor is used—e.g., the purchase of tractors on British farms without reducing the hired staff. Men have always been interested in seeing how work is done in other lands, and in imitating methods superior to their own. The question is what happens to trade as technical change, starting in one country, is diffused throughout the world.

Early demonstration effect and technical assistance took place back and forth across the Channel between Britain and the Continent. Flemish weavers and Lombard bankers instructed the English in their own country, and Arthur Young went to the Low Countries and France in the eighteenth century to study the best agricultural practice. In the nineteenth century the position was reversed. After Waterloo, hundreds of Frenchmen went to Britain to study the Industrial Revolution, and a vast number of British entrepreneurs, foremen, and workmen went to France to teach British techniques to owners and workers.[10] Before the relaxation on the embargo in 1828, machinery was smuggled abroad for imitation.[11]

10. W. O. Henderson, *Britain and Industrial Europe, 1750–1870* (Liverpool, Liverpool University Press, 1954). G. Duveau, *La Vie ouvrière en France sous le second empire* (2d ed. Paris, Gallimard, 1946), p. 126, claims that as many as 16,000 British workers were in France; but B. Gille, *Recherches sur la formation de la grande entreprise capitaliste, 1815–1848* (Paris, S.E.V.P.E.N., 1959), pp. 24–27, believes this number far too large.

11. Oscar Handlin, "International Migration and the Acquisition of New Skills," in B. F. Hoselitz, ed., *The Progress of Underdeveloped Areas* (Chicago, University of Chicago Press, 1952), pp. 54–59.

Technology today spreads in some degree through illegal imitation, including the pirating of design and industrial espionage, but mainly through licensing, direct investment, a simple reading of technical literature, foreign education, and so on. There is little doubt that the speed of diffusion of technology has increased, not only among developed nations but between developed and underdeveloped. There need be no direct communication. That one country can produce a particular article may be sufficient spur to others, as Russian, French, and Israeli work in atomic energy may demonstrate. Technological leadership is harder than ever to maintain, although historians may think it was never held long. The result is that trade based on technical leadership must keep changing, for any given technical gap is foredoomed to closure.

When technical information was diffused only slowly, it could substitute for factor abundance in comparative advantage. The British textile industry had perhaps a slight edge over competition in its access to coal and in the natural air conditioning west of the Pennines, which prevented cotton thread from snapping as readily as elsewhere. These advantages were hardly enough to inhibit the development of competition from a country with really inexpensive labor, such as Japan, once the technology became relatively static in Britain and diffused throughout the world. It is worth noting that Japanese textile manufacturing was not a slavish imitation of Manchester practice—special institutions were devised to recruit and maintain female labor for factory work.[12] But once successful adaptive imitation had been achieved, factor proportions took over from technical superiority as the basis of comparative advantage.

12. W. W. Lockwood, *The Economic Development of Japan: Growth and Structural Change, 1868–1938* (Princeton, 1954).

The same changes in comparative advantage occur today, and at a much faster pace. Transistors are an American invention, and were early exported. But in a comparatively short space of time Japanese production was undertaken, and the United States became a net importer. The position is set forth in Table 6–2.

TABLE 6–2. *Japanese Exports of Transistors and Other Semiconductor Devices to the United States, 1957–1959*

	Transistors		*Other Semiconductor Devices*	
	Quantity (units)	*Value (in thousands of dollars)*	*Quantity (units)*	*Value (in thousands of dollars)*
1957	957	1	Not available	
1958	10,620	7	Not available	
1959	2,393,365	1,581	597,132	92

Source: Japanese Ministry of Finance, *Annual Returns of the Foreign Trade of Japan* (communicated by the Japan-United States Trade Council of Washington, D.C.).

A technical secret may be the basis of trade. Once it is lost, factor proportions may determine which countries export and which import the good. We said "may." It will be recalled from Chapter 4[13] that factor abundance and wage rates are not synonymous with wage costs. MacDougall has said that automobiles are the textiles of today.[14] The implication is that the technology of automobile manufacture is so well known that comparative advantage in the product is no longer based on technology but is a matter of wage and capital costs. It is true that Germany, Britain, France, Italy,

13. See p. 52.

14. G. D. A. MacDougall, "A Lecture on the Dollar Problem," *Economica*, n.s., *21* (1954), 196.

and, to a lesser extent, Sweden (and now the Netherlands) are all exporters, and on the other side of the Iron Curtain so are the Soviet Union, Poland, and Czechoslovakia. But Japan has long tried to manufacture automobiles, with indifferent success until only recently. It is doubtful whether India can do very well in this area. In fact, India has had only a limited success in cotton textiles, partly because of inflation and an overvalued currency, partly for reasons of quality.

THE ANTITRADE BIAS OF IMITATION

Thus far the discussion has run in terms of imitation, in which one country takes over export production from another. This skips an important stage in the analysis in which imitation is antitrade biased. Before an importing country exports, it cares for its own needs without importing. The export stage is by no means always reached. Import substitution occurs more frequently than export creation. Imitation is thus strongly biased against trade.

Recall Burenstam Linder's point that export trade is almost always based on a flourishing home market.[15] The same is true of import substitution. Decreasing costs obtain in many industries up to a certain minimum scale. Rising imports can furnish a sign that the domestic market is sufficiently broad to support a local plant, and that imitation of foreign techniques will pay.[16] Stephen Hymer has noted

15. See above, p. 58.

16. Nurkse, *Some Problems of Capital Formation in Underdeveloped Countries,* pp. 11–17, developed a theory of "balanced growth," based on the narrowness of the domestic market in underdeveloped countries. He held that a new plant producing, say, shoes would have a hard time getting started because the local market for shoes could be readily saturated, and the increased income from more efficient shoe manufacture would be spent not on shoes but on other products. He concluded that

that rubber tire plants are established in any country which reaches a consumption of 50,000 tires a year.[17] As the level of living rises in a developing country, therefore, imports increase in many lines, only to die away again as domestic production takes over. This is particularly true, of course, of market-oriented products such as oil, tires, brewery products, or of footloose ones such as textiles, matches, shoes, apparel.

CLOSING THE TECHNICAL GAP

It looked for a time as though the technical gap between the United States and other developed countries was an enduring feature of international trade. Isolation from the battlegrounds of two world wars, plus an economic history of great labor scarcity relative to land, and later to capital, gave the United States an interest in innovation which was more widespread among the populace and among economic sectors than in other countries.

This view can no longer be held with assurance. The United States lead has been closed in many lines, and even reversed, in the last ten years. One reason for the narrowing of the gap has been technical assistance to Europe in connection with the European Recovery Program with its subsidiary

---

investment in many particular lines would have to wait upon a simultaneous program of investment in all lines, where the increased productivity from each would provide a portion of the necessary market for the others. This theory has been criticized on a number of scores, but not least because it assumes a closed economy. Exports provide a broad market for new industries in many countries that are not limited to domestic sales, and, as indicated in our present text, imports will provide an indication in other lines when the domestic market has reached the appropriate size to warrant a local plant.

17. "The Theory of Direct Investment" (doctoral dissertation, Massachusetts Institute of Technology, 1960), p. 122.

efforts to stimulate productivity. Another is the surge of direct United States investment in Europe. Still another may be the diversion of United States research and development effort into temporarily sterile defense ends, some of which may ultimately yield economically productive by-products.

But there is more to it than these forces, which suggest merely that imitation in Europe and Japan is increasing, and innovation in the United States slowing down. Europe and Japan are innovating positively. Major developments in the particularly American field of innovation—the automobile—have mainly been of European origin: the disc brake, the two-stroke engine, independent springing, and so on.

Particularly interesting is the new spirit of innovation in France, which has produced in the 1950s the Caravelle and the Mystère in airplanes, the Citroën DS 19 and "deux chevaux" (two horsepower) in automobiles, high-voltage long-distance electric transmission, and direct transmission at 25,000 volts to electric locomotives. These and other equally radical departures from simple imitation of leading technical performance suggest a surge of independent innovation in France which is linked in curious ways that social scientists do not understand to the social changes taking place in that country, and helping to produce the improvement in output and in the balance of payments so striking since 1953.

TECHNOLOGICAL CHANGE TO ORDER

Innovations and inventions may or may not fit the requirements of economic progress, including domestic growth, expanding exports and domestic production of goods formerly imported. The Bessemer and Siemens-Martin processes to make steel were as widely employed outside Britain, where they were developed, as inside; and the Thomas process for making steel from phosphatic ores became much more useful abroad than in the Britain of its origin.

These examples are in striking contrast with, say, the Swedish development of the sulphite and sulphate processes for treating pulpwood to make paper. These inventions came forward after 1870 just when they were needed to take advantage of the development in Britain of an enormous appetite for paper, resulting from the penny post, the penny press, and the bureaucratic revolution in government and industry, not to mention the spread of literacy and education. Similarly in Denmark, the conversion of the economy from a grain exporter to a producer of eggs, bacon, and butter for the breakfast tables of England required two innovations: one, the cream separator, to permit the manufacture of butter on an efficient scale instead of by the peasant churn; the other, in the more difficult social field, the cooperative, which made it possible to link the labor-intensive, small-scale production of animal products with the large-scale standardized marketing needed to conquer the rapidly rising British market. The beginnings of cooperatives in Denmark can be found well in advance of the fall of wheat prices after 1879, which stimulated the transformation of the economy to animal products; and still further back are the roots of generalized education among rural folk which made cooperation possible. But the social scientist finds technological and social change which neatly fits the requirements of a market a rare phenomenon and an inexplicable one.

Technical change may then be independent, and linked to noneconomic variables, as in France today; or it may be derivative, the simple process of imitation, which may or may not be adroit and fit the requirements of the economic situation. (When it does not, we run into "technological lags and leads" comparable to "cultural lag" and to the less widely known "cultural lead"—the borrowing of social institutions from a more advanced society that are inappropriate to the existing situation.) The successful production of technical and social change to order, whether in rational response to need or unconsciously, is the highest form of economic and social adaptation.

But technical change has undeniable effects on trade, both creative and destructive. Innovation creates and destroys trade, imitation destroys and sometimes replaces.

7 CAPACITY TO TRANSFORM

THE PERMANENCE OF CHANGE

The world of foreign trade is one of change. It makes a great difference to the trade of different countries, and to the impact of trade on them, whether they are capable of changing with the world. Change is both internal and external. Within a country, at a minimum, population is likely to change. If economic growth occurs, there will also be changes in capital supply and technology, perhaps discovery of new resources and, with luck, growth of income per capita. Change abroad is more certain and likely to be more far-reaching. It occurs in every aspect of demand and supply, of both a country's exports and imports. The question is how a country's foreign trade reacts to change.

Capacity to transform is capacity to react to change, originating at home or abroad, by adapting the structure of foreign trade to the new situation in an economic fashion.

Capacity to expand exports in new lines that are the result of domestic innovation and growth goes without saying and presents no problem. The difficulty arises when the change abroad is of a negative character—a change in taste away from a country's exports, a discovery of competitive sources of supply, a technological change which replaces the natural product previously exported or reduces the demand for it. There is also the question of whether a country can take advantage of favorable change, but not overdo its response. By a favorable change is meant an increase in demand, or a rise in cost of competitive supply, to limit ourselves to changes abroad. The exaggerated response may be more harmful than failure to react. It will be discussed presently. But first we must mention the requirements of transformation.

THE TRANSFORMING SOCIETY

The traditional society is engaged in endless repetition. Consumption and production are carried on in the same way from generation to generation. Much production and consumption proceeds on a subsistence basis outside the market. Change is not absent, but it occurs slowly, and is resisted. Social values dominate economic. The appetite for income is kinked: when social needs are filled, leisure is valued above more goods. Succeeding generations follow in the same occupations, which are determined by social status or caste.

In such a society capacity to transform is limited. Change in the outside world is ignored, as far as possible. Contacts are limited, and their widening is resisted. When price falls, more may be produced of the traditional products to maintain income; when price rises, less. In this instance, the price system will operate perversely. But some economists suggest that the price system is merely irrelevant to the allocation of resources in these primitive economies. This means that such economies have no capacity to transform.

In a transforming society, much has altered. Consumers are interested in increasing real income. Producers specialize and work for the market, exchanging goods against money and money against goods. A higher price leads to more labor, land, and capital being attracted to a given product, and more output. A lower price results in reduced production.

These reactions require responses to profit and to income differences on the part of entrepreneurs and owners of factors which disregard traditional usage. Entrepreneurs are ready to shift to new occupations, labor to take on unaccustomed tasks. There must be occupational, spatial, and probably social mobility to accommodate the shifts of factors required by evolving economic opportunities. Upward social mobility must be possible through economic success, and not only through the army, church, and politics. A minimum of education and literacy are required—more is better—to permit the retraining of labor and its instruction in new tasks.

Transformation does not demand shifts of the whole economy from one task to another. The changes occur at the margin. Profitable industries grow, attracting new entrepreneurs, new supplies of labor, new land, new capital. Industries rendered unprofitable by rising costs, declining demand, or increased competition from more efficient sources of supply lose factors of production and lose their attraction to entrepreneurs. Capital may escape no faster than the rate of depreciation, and older people who have spent their lives in an industry may be unwilling to leave it. But increments in factors, and factors being replaced, are available for entry into the growing industries.

Capacity to transform probably follows a pattern. In traditional societies it is minimal. With exposure to the modern world it increases. At some stage in the growth process it reaches a peak, and then there seems to be some diminution in it. The adage "three generations from shirtsleeves to shirtsleeves" suggests that the third generation has lost its capacity to transform a business that is no longer profitable. Success can go on longer than three generations, as the economic history of some leading Boston families illustrates—first shipping, then whaling and rum, then textiles, then railroad and automobile securities. But there are families which stayed in textiles and in New England mills rather than turn to the new and more efficient mills of the South. Some of these families can be said to have failed to transform.

GROWTH IN TRADITIONAL COMMODITIES

Hla Myint has suggested that direct investment in plantations in the Far East produced a once-and-for-all technical change, which stopped there.[1] Specialization was achieved, together with production for the market, even a transformation, but no capacity to transform on an evolving basis. Myint calls the process "fossilization." One traditional society had been exchanged for another—a more productive one to be sure, but one which a world of change would ultimately turn against. Growth can occur—expansion of the production of the newly traditional commodities. Increments in factor supply will be invested at the margin in the same proportions as the inframarginal factors now available—at least in those countries where additional land is available. But this means that expansion will ultimately go too far,

1. "The Gains from International Trade and the Backward Countries," *Review of Economic Studies*, 22 (1954–55), 129–42.

enlarging the supply and exports even after the marginal return from added exports is less than their cost.

The theory of comparative advantage does not say that increments of factors coming into existence should be invested in exports because the export industries are, on the average, more productive than import-competing industry. Resources should be invested so that they earn the same at the margin in all industries; and an increment of resources should be invested in export, import-competing, or domestic industry depending upon the relative rates of return in each. A nontransforming society, however, will go on investing the incremental resources of a given sector in the same sector. Additions to labor and capital that arise in a profitable industry will continue to be invested in that industry. The sector may run out of land, which will bring the process to a halt. But if it does not, the economy may continue to expand in exports regardless of relative prices among sectors, and of relative profitability. The country will complain that the terms of trade are adverse for primary products, or for underdeveloped countries. The complaint will be true, but the difficulty will lie not in the manipulation of its terms of trade by the world beyond its frontiers, but in its incapacity to transform.

Incapacity to transform may lead to disaster at an earlier stage as a consequence of trade. When trade begins, cheap imports may impinge on a domestic sector engaged, as in early India, in the production of cloth. The price of cloth falls. According to the free-trade model, the factors engaged in cloth production should shift into other more remunerative occupations, with the country as a whole faring better as a result of trade. But they may know no other possibilities. For a time they go on producing at a loss, and finally they are wiped out. In an interesting theoretical modification of the theory of international trade, Gottfried Haberler has suggested that trade could hurt a country if the normal classical assumption of full employment is discarded, and if the factors previously engaged in the import-competing sector are unable to shift into other industries, and become unemployed. In this case the loss through unemployment might be greater than the gain from trade, and a tariff would be justified.[2]

Haberler regarded this possibility of a loss through trade as more a theoretical than a real possibility. The wage of the import-competing labor might be reduced, but this labor would probably not become totally unemployed. But Burenstam Linder raises the question whether this is realistic in underdeveloped economies where factors employed in the import-competing sector are already close to the subsistence wage level.[3] In this circumstance, the problem is not one of pushing a factor into partial or complete unemployment, but of annihilating it. If labor engaged in the import-competing industry is unable to shift to other occupations, and is already at a subsistence wage—assuming that entrepreneurs are not receiving monopoly profits that can be reduced—additional imports lead to the destruction of the factors in the isolated import-competing sector.

The effects of inability to transform on the export sector and on the import-competing sector can be combined. The former sector expands through the growth of population and capital; the latter contracts because of the increase in imports. Even if the country started with fairly balanced resources, it ends with resources skewed. Increased skewness for a time adds real income to the economy—though it is

2. "Some Problems in the Pure Theory of International Trade," *Economic Journal, 60* (1950), 223–40.

3. Linder, *An Essay on Trade and Transformation,* chap. 2.

impossible to judge what happens to welfare when the factors in one sector increase in real income while another sector is wiped out. But unless there is a beginning of capacity to transform, or a limit in the expansion of exports is reached through some constraint, such as lack of land, skewness will increase further. After a time, it begins to add at the margin less than the average return theretofore. Exports may continue to expand even when returns for the economy are negative. The terms of trade turn against the enlarging economy that cannot transform.

This seems to be what the spokesmen for underdeveloped countries have in mind when they complain about the terms of trade facing their countries, and the dangers of overexporting. The gains from trade for a highly specialized country are great. Graham has shown that large countries with wide powers of transformation get little of the gains from trade, because their comparative costs set the prices at which the world trades.[4] And this is generally the case. New entrants into industrial products, minerals, and agricultural commodities produced in the temperate zone can expand their markets at relatively constant prices provided that developed countries withdraw from these occupations as prices tend to decline. But no such cushion exists in "colonial products" which are not produced in the temperate zone developed countries.[5] In these commodities there is no cushion

4. Frank D. Graham, *The Theory of International Values* (Princeton, Princeton University Press, 1948).

5. John Burr Williams, *International Trade under Flexible Exchange Rates* (Amsterdam and New York, 1954), chap. 8, defines colonial products as those that are not consumed in the exporting country. For some purposes this may be the relevant criterion: the product has to be exported, if it is produced at all, because there is no possibility of consuming it at home. But in the present context it is the lack of home production in the importing country that counts. Of course, if developed

of import-competing production in the importing country to keep the price constant whatever the level of output, within limits, at which the underdeveloped countries want to sell.

If producers have no capacity to reallocate resources among industries, increases in output are likely to continue until they saturate markets in the importing countries. If price elasticity is low, the terms of trade will be adverse, and may even deteriorate to the point where they make the country worse off as a result of expansion. Jagdish Bhagwati's model of "immiserizing growth,"[6] in which a country is worse off after growing than before, because the loss in the terms of trade outweighs the gain from increased productivity, has struck many commentators as a curiosity rather than a serious representation of a real case.[7] But this is because the critics have had in mind economies which function according to the price system. If one sector were to grow automatically, because of periodic increases in the supply of factors and inability to transform, and without limit, immiserizing growth would become a real possibility.

The possibility, or prospect, of immiserizing growth very much concerns the underdeveloped countries, especially those of Latin America and the Far East. Much has been made in Latin America of the inelasticity of demand in the

---

countries refuse to reduce domestic production when production expands abroad, and keep out incremental imports by increased tariffs or quotas —as in oil production in the United States today—domestic production in the importing country provides no price stability for the exporter, and all products become "colonial."

6. "Immiserizing Growth: A Geometrical Note," *Review of Economic Studies,* 25 (1958), 201–05.

7. See, for example, Harry G. Johnson, "Economic Development and International Trade," unpublished manuscript representing the substance of two lectures delivered in the Economics Faculty of the University of Copenhagen, April 28 and 29, 1959, mimeographed, p. 9.

United States and Europe for primary products—probably too much, for no attention has been paid to the substantial expansion in primary production that has already taken place with profit, or to the room that remains for further expansion as the developed countries transform further and shift more resources out of import-competing goods. The transformation from an export to an import basis in minerals in the United States has been mentioned, as have the earlier effects of depletion in Europe. The historical and statistical case made by Latin American economists that the terms of trade have consistently run against them is not convincing. Nor is their argument that since the terms of trade will deteriorate, and neither exports nor capital imports can be expanded, they are obliged to cut down imports of consumers' goods in order to be able to purchase the raw materials and capital equipment needed as they grow. But their case derives some support from the fact that, in the past, growth without transformation has not been rewarding.

Two different types of economy exist in the Far East: the sparsely settled rice exporters, such as Burma and Thailand; and the export-oriented plantation sort, such as Ceylon, India, Indonesia, and Pakistan, where population is high and growing and land sets limits to expansion.[8] The problem for the first sort is that population growth is likely to cut off exports, because these are staples of domestic consumption. In the second, problems abound. The first problem concerns the availability of land to expand exports; the second, whether capital formation, in the form of irrigation or the application of fertilizer or machinery, can enlarge capacity. If a

8. Hiroshi Kitamura, "Foreign Trade Problems in Planned Economic Development," a paper submitted to the International Economic Association Round Table on Economic Development, with Special Reference to East Asia, Japan, 1960.

favorable answer is received on either of the first two questions, the issue remains whether the world will take much more jute, burlap, tea, rubber, or coconut oil, to name a few examples. In its *Economic Survey for 1959*, the United Nations Economic Commission for Asia and the Far East estimated that most countries of this area may be expected to increase their export earnings over the next twenty years by about one-half, or a compound rate of 2.05 per cent a year.[9] This may well be less than the increase in population of the area.

COBWEB THEOREM

Worse than not being able to respond to an economic stimulus may be, under certain circumstances, responding too much. This reaction occurs especially when there is a long period of gestation in the production of the commodity, between initial investment and its fruition. In developed countries the cobweb theorem is used to describe excessive response into and out of given lines of production as price goes up and down, with the excessive shift of resources producing a reversal of the price movement and a new movement. Here is capacity to transform with a vengeance. The price of corn rises relative to the price of hogs. Farmers market corn, rather than feed their hogs, to such an extent that deliveries of hogs fall, their price rises relative to that of corn, and the pendulum swings in the other direction.

The classic case in underdeveloped countries concerns coffee in Brazil. Here the difficulty lies in the long length of time it takes the plant to mature. Coffee bushes do not bear their first fruit until five or six years after planting. (If the

9. United Nations Economic Commission for Asia and the Far East, *Economic Survey for 1959*.

production period were short, as in manufactured goods with excess capacity available, a price increase would be dampened immediately by an increase in output.) But in coffee there is not only the time needed to clear land and to plant, but five years to wait after that. The price stays high, and new planting continues. Destabilizing speculation may drive the price higher. And in six to seven years' time, when the harvest is reaped, no fall in price can stop the avalanche of new production, unless it falls below the cost of picking.

In cotton in the United States during the first half of the nineteenth century, price rises became cumulative because the initial response was to divert planters from current production to clearing land, so that higher prices meant an initially smaller crop. The cumulative price rise led to overadjustment and ultimate collapse, even in this single-season crop, because current output and future output were competitors for existing resources.

Such is possibly true of sugar, where the shortage of the 1920s led to the glut of the next decade, and World War II was equally followed by famine and flood.

INCAPACITY TO TRANSFORM IN DEVELOPED ECONOMIES

Underdeveloped economies are not alone in their incapacity to adapt. Just as developed countries experience the cobweb response in residential building and even manufactured products like ships, as well as in primary production, so from time to time and from country to country do they experience difficulty in transforming. Distressed areas, pockets of unemployment, and low-income industries and regions are found in countries of all levels of average income.

The reasons for incapacity to adjust are social in developed countries as well as underdeveloped. In Lowell, Massachusetts, the young do not move away when the cotton mills cut back output; they share the work on short time, or take turns in working full time in the mills and drawing unemployment relief. The green valleys of Wales similarly clung to their youth when coal was depressed in the 1930s. Brittany and the Southwest in France and the South of Italy contain disguised unemployment in agriculture, along with industrial workers at less than average national wage rates who refuse to migrate to increase their earnings. The European Coal and Steel Community tried to move miners from the played-out mines of Aquitaine to the then booming Lorraine area. The effort was not a success. One miner wanted to know how they expected to get the men to move if they did not bring along the cemetery.

The French structure of foreign trade is one of the most insensitive to change. Gérard Salette has made a study of the flexibility of trade structures by dividing the trade of six industrial countries of Europe—Britain, Germany, France, Italy, Belgium, and Sweden—for a selected set of years—1872, 1900, 1913, 1928, 1938, and 1952—into eight classes of goods by percentages. He derived a rudimentary index of flexibility by adding the changes in percentage points from period to period for the five intervals (one less than the number of years) without regard to sign. Thus if food, drink, and tobacco, as a class, comprised 20, 10, and 20 per cent of total exports at three points in time, one would add the −10 and +10 without regard to sign to get an index of 20.[10]

Calculated in this way, the index of flexibility was lower for France than for the other five countries, as shown in Table 7–1.

The measure is by no means perfect, since transformation

10. Gérard Salette, unpublished paper presented at seminar at M.I.T.

TABLE 7–1. *Structural Rigidity in European Trade, 1872–1952 (cumulated percentage points of difference in eight trade commodity groups, five periods)*

France	117.6
Sweden	130.0
United Kingdom	135.0
Germany	158.0
Italy	170.8
Belgium	200.2

Source: Calculated by Gérard Salette, using data set forth in C. P. Kindleberger, *The Terms of Trade* (New York, John Wiley and Technology Press of M.I.T., 1956), pp. 58–61.

can take place within classes, or even within a narrow commodity classification. Moreover, the arithmetic summation is distortionary for some purposes. The position for France is more seriously rigid than the table suggests, because changes in one direction, subsequently reversed, appear as significant as cumulative changes from period to period. In the important field of textiles, for example, the British changes were consistent decreases that amounted to 42 percentage points, or an average of more than 8 per cent a year in the same direction. The French total for the same category was 20.9, but consisted of 15.7 points of decrease and a 5.2 increase between 1913 and 1928 for a net decrease of only 10.2 percentage points over eighty years. Duvaux and Weiller assert that the French foreign trade structure is rigid because French industrial production is inflexible, and also because commercial policy has resisted change.[11] One should

11. Weiller and Duvaux, "Economie française," esp. pp. 24, 50. Professor Weiller has suggested in "Long-Run Tendencies in Foreign Trade, with a Statistical Study of the French Trade Structure, 1871–1939" (preliminary draft of a manuscript of the Economic Department of the League of Nations, made available by courtesy of the author), p. 33, that the conservative character of French postwar reconstruction after World War I was due to the great prestige of the prewar structure.

hasten to add, however, that since about 1953 there has been a great transformation in French exports, with a large expansion of sales of automobiles, petroleum products, aluminum, and even airplanes, as a result of the post-World War II technical renaissance.

TRANSFORMATION AND THE TERMS OF TRADE

Economic transformation by older countries has importance on two scores. It enables them to allocate resources to take advantage of changes in prices and profit opportunities, and it leaves room for underdeveloped countries which can expand only in limited directions. The latter point has been made repeatedly, but is worth fresh emphasis. On the first score, however, it is not always realized that the intense interest of such countries as Britain in their terms of trade has the same origin as those of underdeveloped countries, an implicit acknowledgment that the country does not reallocate rapidly to take advantage of price changes. In a smoothly transforming economy the terms of trade play an important role in guiding the allocation of resources but have limited importance for income distribution. If all factors are continuously reallocated so as to equalize returns at the margin, industries with falling prices uncompensated by increases in relative efficiency lose factors until the decline in production arrests the fall in price and factor return; and industries with rising prices gain resources. If different industries employ factors in differing proportions, there may be some change in the relative demand for factors, which effects some redistribution of income. But this is relatively unimportant compared to the problem of the impact of changes in the terms of trade on "specific" factors—those which have no power to move. If Britain produces what it produces, regardless of price, its terms of trade may be its greatest problem, as some observers have thought. But if resource reallocation can take place in response to price changes, the relationship of export to import prices declines sharply in importance.

Note that the terms of trade should be thought of as adjusted for changes in productivity. The wide fall in the prices of British textiles between 1750 and 1850—by about half—was consistent with an increase in the returns to factors in the textile industry, since productivity more than doubled. Similarly, in the foreign trade of Finland, because timber prices in 1959 were double the 1922 level and paper prices below it, one must not conclude that the timber industry was better off than the paper industry. Actually paper exports expanded four times over the period, and timber exports fell by 10 per cent.[12] But this was because there was little change in productivity in timber and a great increase in paper. The single factoral terms of trade—that is, the relative prices of exports and imports, adjusted for the change in productivity of exports—are the significant variable.

CREATIVE TRANSFORMATION

Occasionally there occur transformations which result from an outside negative stimulus. The Danish response to the fall of the price of wheat, mentioned in the previous chapter—of ceasing to export wheat and instead importing grain for feed for animal products—is one such. A trivial example occurred after World War II in the pecan-shelling industry in the United States, which sought protection to

12. Erkki Laatto, "Terms of Trade and Economic Growth," *Unitas* (Quarterly Review Illustrating Economic Conditions in Finland), no. 4 (1959), 176–81.

defend itself against competition from low-wage labor abroad. When protection was refused, the industry responded by converting from a labor-intensive industry employing marginal female workers in congested areas to a modern industry. Machinery was devised to shell pecans. The industry managed successfully to compete with imports and even to expand sales.

British agriculture, on the other hand, was allowed to collapse after the removal of the Corn Laws in 1846—with a delay. This transformation has been discussed by Karl Polanyi.[13] To Polanyi it was the culminating antisocial act of a society which elevated economic and financial values above social, in that it permitted cheap wheat from overseas to drive 200,000 agricultural workers off the farm in the ten years after 1879. British agriculture did convert to a limited extent from grain to animals. But it is striking that this transformation of agriculture was so limited compared with the reallocation from agriculture to industry. The demand for protective foods—meat, milk, eggs, vegetables—was high and growing, and advantage was taken of it by the farmers of countries around Britain to a far greater extent than those within the country.

Competition from imports can have stimulating effects. Arthur Dunham reaches the conclusion that the Anglo-French Commercial Agreement of 1860 sped the completion of the Industrial Revolution in France, and especially the conversion of iron production from charcoal to coke, and of textiles from handicraft to factory work.[14] A hundred years

13. Karl Polanyi, *The Great Transformation* (New York, Farrar and Rinehart, 1944).

14. *The Anglo-French Treaty of Commerce of 1860 and the Progress of the Industrial Revolution in France* (Ann Arbor, University of Michigan Press, 1930).

later, French economists again look for competitive stimulation from the European Economic Community.[15]

It follows that it is impossible to generalize about the impact of an adverse change in demand or supply abroad. One possible reaction, given the lack of power to transform, is to leave resources where they are and to lose income because of lower prices for exports, or higher prices for imports. A second possibility is to shift resources in response to the change. A third is to respond by innovation either in the same line or in one that takes advantage of the change. But economics is able to tell us very little about the conditions under which given societies will respond in one way or another to the same stimulus.

15. Maurice Allais, *L'Europe unie, route de la prospérité* (Paris, Calmann-Lévy, 1960).

8 RANDOM FACTORS

WAR AND CHANGE

The preceding chapters must not be allowed to leave the reader with the notion that the evolution of a country's foreign trade exclusively follows deep-seated laws based on the growth of factor supplies, the development of technology at home and abroad, and the country's capacity to transform. More than in most aspects of the economy, foreign trade is subject to a wide variety of influences, which, however systematic in some cosmic view of society, must be regarded as outside the economic system, or at least remote from foreign trade and therefore random in incidence. The examples in the classic literature have been crop failures and bumper harvests. More far-reaching have been the effects of revolution and war. Not without influence are pestilence, labor strikes, and similar events outside the realm normally discussed by trade economists. These factors will not occupy us long, but they must be mentioned for the sake of completeness.

War, as just said, is the most far-reaching of these outside events. Social scientists lack a simple theory of the effects of war on economic change. One hypothesis worth testing is that war speeds up all processes, stimulating growth already under way and hastening the aging process where this has begun. But the economic renaissance of Europe after World War II would seem to disprove this theory.

In the history of trade, the Crusades merit attention for widening the horizon of European peoples, and especially traders, breaking open new transport routes, introducing new commodities, terms, even techniques into Western usage. John Condliffe has traced the Arabic origin of such household words as cotton and sugar, and even of the commercial terms traffic and tariff, to the Moorish conquests and the Holy Wars.[1] In modern times there have been the Napoleonic wars, which led to the spread of sugar beets on the Continent and the loss of this market to the West Indies; the Embargo of 1809, which gave a start to the textile industry in New England, a start later supported by the Tariff of 1816; the Civil War in the United States, which spread the cultivation of cotton on a significant scale to Egypt and India; the Korean Conflict, which touched off a boom in raw materials which went too far and evoked a reaction; and possibly the British and French attack on Suez in 1957, which marked the turning point in the position of the United States dollar.

Far more significant, of course, were the two world wars of the twentieth century, the first of which accelerated the

1. *The Commerce of Nations* (New York, 1950), pp. 21, 25.

growth of the economic strength of the United States, while the second saw the introduction of at least three new industries—atomic energy, rocketry, and, on a significant scale, electronics.

War is an incubator of factor growth and technological change, directly and through its impact on foreign trade. It is also the most efficient protective device yet discovered. Direct trade between the warring countries ceases; much other trade is cut off, either by embargoes—such as Napoleon maintained in the Continental system, which forbade the rest of Europe to trade with Britain, or such as the British attempted to enforce between the rest of the world and Napoleon—or by the unavailability of goods. Latin American industrialization twice received stimulation on the demand side from the world wars; European and United States supplies of exports were cut down, leaving room for domestic manufacturers. The difficulty was that equipment and materials needed to meet these demands were also lacking.

The effects of war are not only contemporaneous. Disturbances of an unpredictable nature may subsequently ensue. There is territorial change, such as we discussed earlier for the Austro-Hungarian Empire, and revolutionary shifts of government, such as occurred in Russia in 1917 and in China in 1949. After World War II, the defeated or subverted countries of Eastern and Central Europe had their entire economies, including their foreign trade, transformed.

A consequence of war with particular effects on trade is reparations. These were disturbing only in the short run after 1870. In the 1920s they were far more seriously upsetting. Reparations in kind posed one sort of problem—competition for normal foreign trade. British coal exporters disliked German reparation in that commodity. Monetary reparations gave rise to a more profound disturbance of international monetary conditions, especially after foreign lending from the United States ceased to facilitate their payment. Reparations in Western Europe were carried to no great extent after World War II, so great were the problems of reconstruction and trade restoration to which lend-lease, postwar grants, and ultimately the Marshall Plan made important contributions. In Eastern Europe the Soviet Union levied heavy obligations in reparations on the defeated allies of Germany, but final portions of payment had to be canceled to prevent the economic collapse of the debtors. The effects of reparation on Finland, which met its entire obligation, were particularly striking. Seventy-two per cent of the $500 millions of reparations were exacted in metal and engineering products, creating an entirely new industry in excess of Finnish needs, and dependent, after the end of reparations, on export markets in the Soviet Union.

PESTILENCE

Disease is less directly man-made than war but has had a surprisingly great impact on international trade. Whatever may have been the effects on trade of the Black Death—which economic historians hold responsible in significant degree for the emergence from the Middle Ages, through the necessity to change production methods after the loss of so much manpower—plant and animal diseases have had direct effects on international trade in modern times. Perhaps the most striking examples are those of pébrine and phylloxera, both in France. The first was the disease of the silkworm, which sharply reduced the production of silk in the 1850s and led to subsequent imports from Japan and China to support the silk manufacturing industry of Lyons.

Phylloxera was a plant pest which struck the vineyards of France after 1875, reducing acreage and production, cutting off exports which had benefited from the Anglo-French Treaty of 1860, leading to imports from Spain and Italy, stimulating production in Algeria, and converting a bulwark for the free-trade policies of Napoleon III into a supporter of tariffs. The changes in French foreign trade in silk and wine are shown in Table 8–1. Perhaps more significant but

TABLE 8–1. *French Trade in Wine and Raw Silk, 1847–1896 (annual averages by decades, by volume)*

	Wine (in thousands of hectoliters)			*Raw Silk*
	Exports	*Imports*	*Net Exports (− = net imports)*	*Imports (in metric tons)*
1847–56	1,733	94	1,639	3,100
1857–66	2,160	183	1,977	5,800
1867–76	3,235	406	2,829	9,075
1877–86	2,698	6,417	−3,719	10,540
1887–96	1,951	9,287	−7,336	12,010

Source: aggregated from Direction Générale des Douanes, *Tableau Décennal du Commerce, 1867 à 1876* (Paris, Imprimerie National, 1878) and *1887 à 1896* (Paris, Imprimerie National, 1898).

not reducible to tabular form were the resulting changes in political sentiment. Wheat farmers, textile manufacturers (with a few exceptions), and coal and iron interests were protectionist and opposed the program of tariff reductions through treaties which began in 1860. Support for the treaties came from the exporters—from Lyons' silk manufacturing, Rhone and Bordeaux vineyards, the luxury trades of Paris, and the cotton textile industry of Alsace. When pébrine, phylloxera, and the loss of Alsace to Germany in the Treaty of Frankfort struck three out of four of these interests, it seemed as though the Lord had ordained that France should revert to protectionism.[2]

Such far-reaching effects are not found in other diseases, although hoof-and-mouth disease, rabies, and horse sleeping sickness limit trade among some countries in particular products. A happier experience with animal disease occurred in Australia recently. Myxamytosis, the rabbit disease, was introduced into Australia in 1950 and killed off millions of jack rabbits. The setback to this pest freed a vast amount of grass for sheep grazing, increased wool output in a short space of time by as much as 30 per cent, and assisted wool as a crop in meeting the increasing competition from artificial fibers after World War II.

THE VARIABILITY OF HARVEST

Bumper crops and failures play an important role in short-term changes in foreign trade and the balance of payments which cannot be ignored by forecasters and others interested in year-to-year change. Their effects may extend further. The Irish potato famine of 1846 (and a short crop in wheat in Britain and France) sparked the repeal of the Corn Laws, although there were deep-seated influences at work to the same end. (Social science fails to tell us when,

2. See Dunham, *The Anglo-French Treaty*. The parallel between the free-trade movement under Napoleon III and that in the United States after 1934 is compelling. Both proceeded under the executive powers of the central government and would have been difficult to legislate at each step. Both relied on the most-favored-nation clause. In one respect the French program went further than present United States policy, which has refused to provide special support for industry adversely affected by imports. France had a fund of 40 million francs ($8 million of 1860 purchasing power) which was used for loans to firms adversely affected by the treaty. All loans were repaid except one to a coal mine near Bordeaux which went bankrupt.

if at all, the *causa causans* would produce the result, had not the *causa proxima* gone into operation.) The same weather conditions in France in 1846, producing the highest wheat price in fifty years, followed by a bumper crop and the lowest price over the same period, contributed significantly to the discontent that led to the Revolution of 1848 in France.

But there is no need to go so far afield. Illustrations abound. In a dry country like Spain, with a highly variable crop, the weather determines the balance of payments, or comes very close to it. H. D. White observes that "sudden and sharp changes in merchandise movements" in the balance of payments of France before World War I were due not to banking phenomena or general price changes but to poor domestic harvests in 1891, 1894, 1898, 1903, and 1911.[3] The 1934 and 1936 droughts in the United States produced a substantial decline in exports of lard and substantial imports of corn from Argentina.

Failure to recognize the impact of weather on the balance of payments may lead to mistakes of policy. Big harvests in the First Indian Five-Year Plan (1950–55) led observers to think the plan had produced a large increase in food output. The relative crop failure of 1958 leading to a doubling of imports of "food, drink, and tobacco" made it appear that the result may rather have been attributable to a good monsoon. Expanded outputs in 1959 and 1960, however, leave it unclear whether the long-run trend is satisfactorily upward or whether India has benefited from a streak of good weather again in 1959 and 1960, as in 1954 to 1957. The figures illustrating the connection between grain output and the balance of payments are shown in Table 8–2. A similar confusion of the effects of crop variations with trends occurred in Eu-

3. Harry D. White, *The French International Accounts, 1880–1913* (Cambridge, Mass., 1933), pp. 139 ff.

TABLE 8–2. *Indian Grain Production and Trade in Food, 1950–1960*

	Index of Grain Production (1950 = 100)	Imports of Food, Drink, and Tobacco	Net Exports of Food, Drink, and Tobacco (— = net imports)
		(in millions of rupees)	
First Plan: 1950	100	981	326
1951	91	2,490	−955
1952	91	1,654	−304
1953	101	789	684
1954	119	1,048	770
1955	115	391	1,111
Second Plan: 1956	115	167	1,307
1957	121	980	941
1958	108	2,087	281
1959	130		
1960	124		

Source: Grain production: Reserve Bank of India, *Bulletin* (October 1960); trade: United Nations *Yearbook of International Trade Statistics, 1950–58*.

rope in the first year of the Marshall Plan. The 1948 balance of payments of Europe showed a remarkable improvement over 1947, which many observers attributed to the fact that the Marshall Plan had begun on April 3, 1948, and some transitional assistance had been accorded before that. But much more significant was the fact that the 1947 harvest was a very poor one, after deep frost in the winter, floods in spring, and drought in the summer, and 1948 was a good agricultural year. The difference in the harvests between the two years brought about a sharp drop in the need for food imports.

These examples illustrate one important aspect of the relationship between the bounty of nature and imports. They are inversely correlated. A big crop cuts imports, and a small crop expands them. In an agricultural subsistence economy or (what amounts to the same thing) an underdeveloped country recovering from the devastation of war, an increase in national income, in contrast to normal multiplier theory, may produce a reduction in imports rather than an increase. Table 8–3 shows that this happened in Greece from 1950 to 1952. After that date, however, the normal positive correlation between national income and imports reasserted itself, and imports rose faster than income.

TABLE 8–3. *National Income and Imports in Greece, 1950–1958 (in billions of drachmae, and in percentages)*

	Income	*Imports*	*Imports as Percentage of Income*
	(in billions of drachmae)		
1950	24.6	6.4	26
1951	29.2	6.0	20.5
1952	30.3	5.2	17
1953	41.0	7.2	17.5
1954	47.8	9.9	21
1955	54.6	11.5	21
1956	63.9	13.9	22
1957	69.5	15.7	22.5
1958	73.2	16.9	23

Source: International Monetary Fund, *International Financial Statistics,* various issues.

STRIKES

Strikes may both originate in the balance of payments and have effects on trade. The British General Strike of 1926, in particular, resulted from the attempt to force down real wages, as a consequence of the return of sterling to par in 1924 at an overvalued rate. The rate hurt exports and helped imports. The former could be sustained only by cutting wages, or holding wages down while increasing productivity. Strikes started in the coal mines and spread into a general strike of all labor. The General Strike was lost.

While the 1926 strike may have had an umbilical connection with foreign trade in Britain, its impact on, say, United States coal exports was entirely fortuitous. Until that time, coal was a commodity that moved in international trade mainly within hemispheres. A small amount of British coal got the advantage of backhaul rates to Argentina, Australia, and island coaling stations about the world. More was sold as bunkers to ships with home ports in other corners of the world, a transhemispheric export trade in which the consumer fetched the product. A very small amount of Welsh anthracite crossed the Atlantic to sell to Beacon Hill residences in Boston for burning with a fine ash in drawing room fireplaces. But so heavy is coal that even this quality product could compete with American production only at a long distance from the mines, and within trucking distance of the docks.

Immediately after wars, however, and during the British coal strike of 1926, the United States found itself selling coal to Europe. Table 8–4 gives an idea of the amounts; the 1929 and 1939 figures were normal and may have represented bunkers or ballast. After 1947, however, improved mechanization in United States mining, further depletion in Euro-

TABLE 8–4. *United States Bituminous Coal Exports to Europe, for Selected Years, 1920–1947 (in short tons)*

1920	14,627,000
1921	5,478,000
1926	15,760,000
1929	567,000
1939	165,000
1945	3,916,000
1946	16,065,000
1947 (est.)	33,000,000

Source: J. A. Krug, *National Resources and Foreign Aid* (Washington, D.C., Oct. 9, 1947), p. 50.

pean mines, and low freight rates made American coal competitive at many points in Europe.

A more recent shift in the direction of trade was produced by the United States steel strike in 1959. Table 8–5 shows

TABLE 8–5. *Net Exports of Iron and Steel from the United States by Months, 1957–1960*
(excluding advanced manufactures; in thousands of short tons)

Year	*Jan.*	*Feb.*	*March*	*April*	*May*	*June*	*July*	*Aug.*	*Sept.*	*Oct.*	*Nov.*	*Dec.*
1957	809	844	1,238	1,113	1,096	1,049	947	919	925	862	922	569
1958	607	430	514	508	507	306	140	138	194	250	237	35
1959	145	184	165	74	95	105	108	164	32	28	−84	77
1960	18	129	259	367	674	712	695					

Source: United States Department of Commerce, *Survey of Current Business* (February issues, 1958–61).

net exports of iron and steel, after the exclusion of advanced manufactures, and changes within a range from 1,100,000 tons of net exports to net imports of 84,000 tons. The strike lasted from July 15 to November 7, 1959. The impact on trade was of longer duration, as orders were placed abroad in anticipation of difficulty, and continued to be met after it was over. If it were possible readily to eliminate net exports to the Western Hemisphere from the figures, which cannot easily be done on a monthly basis, the change in net exports to the rest of the world, mainly Western Europe and Japan, would be even more dramatic.

It is an ancient methodological question in history whether the contingencies overwhelm the uniformities. In economics, the contingencies or random elements get short shrift as the student is taught always to look for generalities. But it is well to be reminded, occasionally, that from time to time the arbitrary and unpredictable take over and dominate the scene.

9 INTERFERENCE WITH TRADE IN PRIVATE-ENTERPRISE ECONOMIES

MONOPOLY

The analysis thus far has rested on the assumption of competition among producers and consumers. But this is not inevitably so. Control over supply by one or more producers, or control of demand by one or more purchasers, may raise or lower the price above or below the competitive level and result in higher or lower than normal profits in the industry. There may be discrimination in the prices charged to various buyers or obtained from various suppliers. There may be, in short, monopoly, monopsony (buyer monopoly), or monopolistic or imperfect competition.

Controversy exists over the extent and the effects of interference in market competition. Some contend that this interference is relatively ineffective, and that, for the most part, and in the not very long run, profits tend to be equalized between industries; and it is held that monopolies fail to distort significantly either the allocation of resources or the volume of trade. However, there is a wide literature, extending from the Marxist views, on the one hand, to those of the "liberal" antitrust adherents, on the other, which finds the effects of monopoly revealed everywhere. One particularly important body of opinion in international economics considers that developed countries sell at monopoly prices and underdeveloped countries at competitive or monopsonistic prices, the result being to depress the latter's terms of trade, gains from trade, and real income.

The subject is vast, and space permits us only to sketch its broad outlines.

There are some "natural monopolies" based on the existence of imperfectly elastic demands and limited supplies. The two that come first to mind in international trade are diamonds for jewelry, and nickel. The demand for jewelry is certainly inelastic with respect to price: it may even be perverse with a larger quantity being demanded at higher prices rather than lower—in the present range. The imperfect elasticity of the demand for nickel comes from the fact that there are no ready substitutes at the price at which it sells, and the amount of nickel in most products is small relative to their selling price. Most derived demands are similarly imperfectly elastic.

Supply is limited in both diamonds and nickel by the restricted incidence of the commodities in the natural state, and as a result of the efforts of the De Beers diamond syndicate and the International Nickel Company to control the marketing of such production as takes place. Where the De Beers syndicate does not own diamond mines, it makes arrangements to market output for the owners on generous terms. I.N.C.O. owns the major world source of nickel in Canada, and one or more other mines such as those in New Caledonia. Its Petsamo mines in Finland were taken over by the Soviet Union at the end of the Finnish war in 1942.

There are limits to natural monopoly, both in demand and supply. An imperfectly elastic demand is not inelastic for every price from zero to infinity. As the price gets higher the elasticity increases. Elasticity also increases with time, as consumers find it worthwhile in the long run to employ substitutes. And very abnormal profits will ultimately stimulate new entry of substitute products.

RESTRAINT OF TRADE

Simple monopolies on a world scale based on the idiosyncracy of nature are rare. The monopoly problem in international trade is caused largely by two or more companies acting together to limit output or marketings and holding up price. They may agree on a course of action, or they may simply act independently but with a sensitive awareness of what the others would like them to do—called "conscious parallel action" by the United States Supreme Court. Or there are limits to entry other than natural scarcity: patents, which are unavailable to the potential competition—nylon for a time, chemicals and pharmaceuticals, electronic equipment; or the process may demand such an enormous amount of capital for production on an efficient scale that new entrants are discouraged—aluminum, copper, international oil, and international iron ore are examples. Some monopolies are natural but local, being maintained by the high cost of shipping bulky or heavy products. This has been the case with cement, oil, coal, and steel but is becoming less and less so because of the decline in transport costs. Finally, in industries with high overhead costs and therefore large room for price cutting in depression, there is powerful pressure for agreements. For such agreements to be successful, all possible competitors must be included, and the agreement must be policed, since there are strong temptations to undercut price and extend sales. It may be necessary to have government support to maintain agreements—either tariffs, to prevent nonparticipants from abroad from upsetting price, or government surveillance, as in shipping and air transport cartels.

A special problem of monopoly in international trade is dumping, or price discrimination among international markets. Many years ago, Viner asserted that there were three types of dumping—sporadic, persistent, and predatory.[1] The sporadic came from the attempt to clear the market of temporary gluts—to sell excess production abroad, far from the normal market, and thus to avoid the necessity of lowering price at home. Persistent dumping arises from selling at one price at home and another abroad, and occurs when a producer can cover more than his average variable costs in the lower-priced market, thus contributing something to overall profits. Typically the home market is the higher-priced market in which the producer tries to cover his overhead costs. But the discrimination may run the other way if the company feels obliged to serve its domestic customers at steady prices, or is required to do so by domestic price controls, and can take advantage of temporary shortages abroad to sell there at higher prices. The company or cartel may have an imperfectly elastic demand abroad and face competition at home. It has long been alleged that before World War I German coal producers sold coal abroad at higher

1. Jacob Viner, *Dumping: A Problem in International Trade* (Chicago, 1923), p. 23.

prices than at home (after allowance for the higher costs of transport), while German steel producers dumped the other way, charging less in the competitive markets abroad, while preserving monopoly prices at home. The evidence, however, is not very persuasive.

Predatory dumping allegedly occurs when a company or industry sells abroad cheaply in an effort to prevent competition from getting a start or to crush it after it is under way, the idea being to raise prices back to their regular or even a monopoly level after the dirty work has been done. Every new industry is persuaded that its competitors are dumping against it, from the textile producers in France and the United States after the Napoleonic wars, to the knit-glove industry of New York State today. But successful predatory dumping demands that a firm once driven out cannot re-enter. There must be an asymmetry between easy exit and difficult re-entry. It is not impossible for this condition to exist, for example, when one competitor gets the jump on the others in an industry with long-run falling cost curves, as Rockefeller is alleged to have done in the oil business in the nineteenth century. Small firms get driven out, and ultimately it is necessary to have a big firm to get back in. But the prevalence of predatory dumping is doubtless exaggerated, especially in such industries as textiles where re-entry is as easy, as a rule, as exit.

There is no agreement on the extent of these practices or on their importance. A number of countries, including Canada and the United States, have special tariffs against dumping. The Federal Trade Commission has asserted that an international oil cartel exists; this is also the view of Representative Wright Patman from Texas, who accused the cartel of dumping in the United States. The Economic Commission for Europe claimed that the price of oil had been held at monopoly levels in Europe. The facts are difficult to disentangle, impossible to present concisely, and debated, if not debatable. What is clear, however, is that profits have been substantial in the oil business, especially on operations outside the United States, and that this has encouraged more and more companies to go into foreign exploration and development. The profits, moreover, have been in the production of crude oil rather than in refining and marketing, but the vertically integrated companies with refining and distribution facilities abroad have been in a better position to dispose of their crude oil than those without such outlets, who have been faced with a serious problem of what to do with their oil once produced. Restrictions on sale to the United States, taken in the name of national defense, close down a once promising avenue. And recently the market in Europe and Africa has been disturbed by the appearance of Soviet surpluses in foreign markets.

There are considerable difficulties in ascertaining the facts about prices in trade that takes place in direct dealings between firms rather than in organized markets. But the major obstacle to the formation of national or international policy is that when the conditions of imperfect competition exist, two rules of conduct for private enterprise come into conflict: maximize profit and eschew discrimination. If any of the demand curves facing an individual firm or group of firms is imperfectly elastic over the relevant portion, the firm can maximize its profits by charging higher prices to those customers whose demand is more inelastic—profit maximization but with discrimination. And under these conditions nondiscrimination means a failure to maximize profit.

Various attempts have been made to draw up rules of conduct for private firms in international trade: by the draft charter of the stillborn International Trade Organization, in the Economic and Social Council of the United Nations, in the General Agreement on Tariffs and Trade, in the European Coal and Steel Community, in the European Economic Community, and so on. Ultimately, however, the dilemma that these two rules of conduct cause leads to breakdown. Cartels and conspiracies among firms may be outlawed. But the virtual impossibility of legally defining what a cartel is makes action rare. The Rome treaty of the European Economic Community, for example, forbids the replacement of tariff barriers by cartels, but no interference with agreements between firms in the same industry in different countries has taken place. If Simca arranges to market Fiat products in France, and Renault to market Volkswagens, this could or could not imply restraint of trade. It is theoretically impossible to tell in advance, and practically impossible to do so afterward.

We are thus left in an unsatisfactory position: we do not know how extensive restraint of trade is in international commerce, nor what its consequences are. It is believed that monopsony among private firms is relatively unimportant, but there is disagreement as to the prevalence of monopoly. Even if we knew all the facts, it is far from self-evident that economists could agree on a policy prescription. Edward Mason has suggested that the cartel problem is relatively unimportant, but he has laid down what many people regard as rather stringent rules for the registration of business agreements, and the exclusion of agreements over the division of markets and the prohibition of limitations on entry.[2] The draft charter of the International Trade Organization and the Economic and Social Council of the United Nations both held that cartels were a serious menace but failed to devise

2. Edward S. Mason, *Controlling World Trade: Cartels and Commodity Agreements* (New York and London, 1946), pp. 2–10.

any method for treating them. An even more difficult task would be to prescribe rules to ensure that international corporations always maximized, buying in the cheapest market and selling in the dearest, both regarded from the short-run point of view. If an American corporation shuts back low-cost production abroad in preference to high-cost capacity at home, it may be maximizing over some long-run period of time, as it attempts to forestall political action to keep out imports or to keep its employees happy where they have the most political power, but it is not maximizing in the sense of a perfect competitor.

STATE TRADING

Not all monopolies or even very large-scale enterprise in free-enterprise economies are private firms. State trading in a socialist system is the subject of the next chapter. But private-enterprise economies have a considerable admixture of governmental trade—armaments, for one thing, and in Europe frequently tobacco, and occasionally alcohol and matches. The first is the result of governments' responsibilities in defense; the latter of the desire to protect important sources of taxation. State liquor authorities are not unknown in the United States, but Sweden prides itself on the acumen of its wine purchasers, who compete with private dealers. Governments also trade electric power produced by nationalized industry or provincial and state authorities.

In addition to the "traditional" government monopolies, however, there has been a considerable degree of state trading and bulk purchase during and immediately after World War II. Some economists thought it desirable to elevate the expedient into a principle. Limitations of foreign exchange and shipping, plus the need to save manpower, were responsible for state trading and bulk purchase during war and reconstruction. There was also an element of monopoly selling and monopsony buying. The arguments for the perpetuation of the system rested on economies of scale. If foreign producers, for example, had assured markets in governmental bulk-purchase contracts, they could cease to worry about the marketing problem and could concentrate on efficient production, passing on part of the gains in efficiency to the consumer in lower prices.

Few countries could be content, however, to allow foreign governments to deal directly with private producers in important markets without intervention: such foreign governments might yield to the temptation of the large buyer to squeeze down prices, and improve their terms of trade. This called for organization on the selling side. With buyer and seller organized, there resulted bilateral monopoly, for which there is no determinate economic solution, and which frequently results in stalemate, and always complaint. Shortly after the war, Argentine shipments of meat to England were interrupted for seven months in one dispute about the appropriate price. British-Danish negotiations were frequently exacerbated, especially during the time of the Korean Conflict boom in raw materials which raised Danish feed costs but did not lead to a revision of British contracts for purchasing eggs, butter, and bacon. In 1951 the Conservative government began the liberalization of trade and its return to private hands. Today there is little support for a return to bulk purchase.

More long-lived than bulk purchase and sale as the result of commercial considerations is the necessity to correct the mistakes of domestic agricultural policy by selling surplus agricultural products abroad. United States practice in this regard is gradually becoming established as a permanent feature of this country's farm and trade policies, and there is even talk—still ironic?—of extending the principle to giving away industrial products to assist in the maintenance of domestic employment and not just for foreign aid.

International trade in armaments is large-scale business, and not only in the Soviet bloc. In the North Atlantic Treaty Organization some standardization and specialization have taken place. Prior to these arrangements each country was supposed to provide for its own defense with a full range of the necessary weapons. Some specialization took place based on factor proportions and location principles: France had the larger ground army, Britain the larger navy. But "buy at home" was the rule. Only lately has it occurred to closely allied governments that there are gains in efficiency available here as well. Atomic energy research is being pursued in more than one country for reasons of prestige and governmental trade in fissionable materials; but increasing specialization is taking place in missiles, various types of aircraft, ground weapons, and standard matériel, with an evident increase in total efficiency.

COMMERCIAL POLICY

The major interference by the state in trade, in private-enterprise economies, however, has been by means of tariffs, subsidies, quantitative restrictions, and exchange regulations. Trade has been left in private hands, but the state has laid down conditions under which it can be carried on. All these interferences, but especially tariffs and embargoes, have an ancient history. Under mercantilism, trade was regarded as a means of improving the state's power, which was related to the size of the country's gold stock. Tariffs were imposed to yield an export surplus and a gold inflow. Navigation acts reserved trade with the colonies for the mother country. An incidental purpose of trade was to strengthen the merchant marine. This meant subsidies for carrying trade in national bottoms or penalties against the use of foreign ships.

In this limited space we can evidently do little more than list the various purposes served by state interference in trade, and to give an idea of their present importance, actual or potential.

REVENUE

One of the oldest purposes of levying tariffs was for the sake of financing government expenditure, the king's customs. It is still not without importance, especially in underdeveloped countries. In the United States, tariffs on imported goods produced 90 to 95 per cent of the federal revenue in 1850; the figure today is below 2 per cent, a figure fairly representative of the order of magnitude of most developed countries which can afford, by and large, to ignore the revenue considerations of tariffs.[3] But underdeveloped countries pay more attention to import and export taxes. Where bookkeeping and accounting are not fully developed in the business community, it is easier to tax goods than incomes. In international trade, moreover, goods are subjected typically to the constriction of a port or border crossing. Smuggling provides an exception to this statement, and is stimulated by

3. Not entirely, for there is an interesting question of current importance: how to divide the customs duties among the governments taking part in a customs union. If the country of entry retains the proceeds, countries like Germany which import through entrepôt towns in other countries (Antwerp and Rotterdam) suffer. On the other hand, to worry about the ultimate destination of the goods is to require surveillance of goods crossing the mutual borders, and record-keeping of a sort that the customs union was intended to eliminate.

tariffs, prohibitions, and export taxes. This used to be an important profession along the French-Swiss and Swiss-Italian borders, as an examination of the statistics of mutual trade reported on both sides indicates. The peak of modern smuggling, however, has been in Indonesian exports to Singapore subject to an export tax; reported imports into Singapore are a sizable multiple of the exports measured in Indonesia.

Too much attention to protection hurts revenue: the prohibitive tariff fills no coffers. And the British found when they moved to free trade between 1846 and 1860, retaining revenue tariffs on only a few items of consumption—sugar, tobacco, tea, spirits, wine, beer—that total revenue from the tariff rose sharply.

SPECIAL INTERESTS

State interference in trade is usually undertaken in behalf of special interests with political power—a class (such as the landowners, the industrialists, the peasantry), a region, an industry, or, in rare cases, a firm. In most instances, the groups concerned attempt to identify themselves with the national interest, wrapping the flag around their financial ambitions, as it were, and adducing the national defense, or the infant-industry argument, or unemployment, as the major reason for curtailing imports or expanding exports. In some cases they may act from the highest of motives. But typically the tariff is sought because competition hurts, prices are lower than they might be, profits are down.

It is not necessary to expatiate on these cases. In the United States, historically it has been the textile, iron and steel, and chemical industries that have sought protection; and more recently producers of petroleum, lead and zinc, watches, bicycles, and textiles have urged increases in old levels of protection, which they claim have become insufficient. An attempt is always made to suggest that increased imports are the cause of the industry's difficulty, but it is frequently evident to outsiders that an important element of internal weakness exists—either an ancient industry in decline (watches in Waltham, textiles in New England), depletion of old mineral deposits (oil, lead and zinc), or a change in taste (favoring the foreign lightweight over the domestic heavy bicycle). The foreigner is a convenient scapegoat.

The special interest may be an entire factor of production, which explains why there are movements to free trade that most economists identify with the general interest. The commercial classes of Manchester in Britain in the first half of the nineteenth century wanted to get rid of the Corn Laws because cheaper bread would make it possible to hold down wages and more imports would expand the market for textile exports. Similarly the gradual support for the Reciprocal Trade Agreements Act in the United States after 1934 came from the large-scale, mass-product exporters, the producers of automobiles, agricultural machinery, and business machines. Or the special interests may ignore the general interest and wield their political power. In Australia, labor is interested in keeping out labor-intensive goods in order to maintain prices on domestic labor-intensive goods and to keep up the level of wages; in Canada, labor claims that tariffs are needed to provide jobs, in the presence of capital-intensive imports, and to stop the emigration to the United States.[4] An industry may be divided, as in oil, between the

4. C. L. Barber, "Canadian Tariff Policy," *Canadian Journal of Economic and Political Science, 21* (1955), 513–30; also J. H. Young, *Canadian Tariff Policy* (Ottawa, Royal Commission on Canada's Economic Prospects, 1957).

large international companies with overseas production, which favor free trade (imports) and the domestic producers who want to maintain the price of domestic production.

A special word is due agriculture. It is widely felt that the rules of competitive enterprise which apply in industry and services are unsatisfactory in this sector. The European Economic Community and the European Free Trade Area both recognize a need to establish a special regime for it. In countries with domestic systems of price stabilization for agriculture it is manifestly impossible to permit imports freely, or the country would find itself supporting the prices of the whole world; and price supports in an exporting country must be offset by subsidies to the extent of "normal" exports, unless the country in question is to raise the world price and encourage new entry abroad.

The argument for special treatment for agriculture is sometimes put in terms of the elasticities; the sector is alleged to be inelastic in supply for decreases in price, though elastic for increases, setting limits to long-run increases in price but none to decreases. Occasionally the argument is put in terms of the inelasticity of demand for price decreases, but not, save for periods of war and reconstruction, for increases, again setting limits. More important, there is technological progress in agriculture; and there is Engel's law, which suggests that as countries grow richer they produce more and consume proportionately less food. Since the political power of a group shifts less rapidly than its economic significance, the farm bloc in most polities is more powerful now than it is likely to be in the future, and it trades heavily on an alleged national need to preserve the family farm and rural virtue.

Under free trade, Britain imported two-thirds of its foodstuffs, produced one-third at home. With the new regime for agriculture, instituted after the war partly for reasons of national defense and partly as a more general aspect of income stabilization, the proportions have shifted to 50/50. Germany, which has much the same general structural outline as an economy, is much more self-sufficient in food. In a closely reasoned argument Liesner asserts[5] that the traditional support given by German tariffs to the farmers since Bismarck's 1879 tariff on "wheat and iron"[6] has accounted for the higher per capita income in Britain than in Germany. Germany produced at home in the mid-1950s 57 per cent of its bread grains (as opposed to 20 per cent for Britain), 83 per cent of its sugar (Britain, 29 per cent), 94 per cent of its meat (Britain, 57 per cent), and 94 per cent of its butter (Britain, 10 per cent). The German agricultural sector locks up a large number of relatively unproductive but politically powerful peasants, and acts as a drag on the highly efficient industrial sector.

THE NATIONAL INTEREST

National defense has been used as an argument to justify tariffs as far back as Adam Smith and even further back, via the gold war chest, to the mercantilists. It continues to be used. The dyestuffs and explosives industries in the United States got their starts in this way, as well as the precision instrument and optical goods industries in both Britain and

5. *The Import Dependence of Britain and Western Germany: A Comparative Study*, esp. chap. 4.

6. The tariff was initially imposed in behalf of the Junkers (for grain) who were at the same time militarists, bureaucrats, and wheat farmers. It was contrary to what would have been the real long-run interests of the peasantry if they had been prepared to shift from the production of grain to livestock, as in Denmark. See Alexander Gerschenkron, *Bread and Democracy in Germany* (Berkeley, 1943).

the United States. Some considerable element of agricultural protection in Britain rests on this basis; and India, the Soviet Union, and doubtless many other countries hold that it is somehow safer in an uncertain world to provide the basic necessities at home. However satisfactory it was in the late Victorian period for Britain to live with only six weeks' supply of food in storage and distribution in the Isles, and another six weeks each unloading in the ports and afloat on the seven seas, national leaders in today's uncertain world want to have food, however expensive, grown domestically, where it can be turned to in crisis.

An intellectual argument for tariffs relates to the improvement in the terms of trade that a country can obtain. A tax on imports will make them obtainable on cheaper terms, provided that the foreign suppliers have a less than perfectly elastic supply schedule. If the United States raises the tax on Swiss watch imports and Switzerland is dependent on the American market, the latter will sell virtually the same number of watches as before but at a lower price. The result is the same as if the United States had taxed Swiss watch manufacturers. Beyond a certain point, however, the loss in volume will outweigh the improvement in the terms of trade and leave the importing country worse off.

It is true that tariffs improve the terms of trade, but this is seldom their purpose. A tariff for protection fails if the foreigner pays the whole duty. The same quantity imported leaves the domestic price unchanged and benefits no domestic producer.

Countries have imposed export taxes, however, to raise the price to the foreigner, and have burned surplus supplies of wheat, or dumped redundant coffee in the ocean, for the same purpose. Moreover, the imposition of export quotas for the purpose of restraining inflation at home has sometimes misfired through exacting a monopoly gain at the expense of the foreign customer while leaving the domestic producer unaffected. Thus, while economists have long recognized that it is possible to improve the terms of trade with tariffs—at least in the short run when demand and supply schedules are relatively inelastic—and the technique has occasionally been urged on the authorities, it is doubtful that the result has been achieved except unintentionally as a by-product, and one not always welcome.

There is even some doubt whether Nazi Germany under the economic leadership of Schacht and Clodius in the 1930s set out deliberately to squeeze their suppliers. They achieved this effect; but their purpose was to permit expansion of national income to be accompanied by expanding trade when the country lacked the foreign exchange reserves to take the risks of trading unilaterally. A clearing system was devised to make trade possible. Once it had been established, Germany had strong incentives to import, but not to export; and to pay any necessary price in foreign currency to obtain imports, but to charge still higher prices for grudgingly ceded exports. The exploitation stumbled upon in this way led Albert Hirschman to explore how much one country could exploit another through the fact of the latter's dependence. He used an index, running from 100 when a country's exports go solely to one national customer to very low numbers when a country's trade is evenly divided among a large number of countries.[7] Table 9–1 suggests that there are con-

7. *National Power and the Structure of Foreign Trade* (Berkeley, 1945). The measure is the Gini coefficient, which is the square root of the sum of the squares of the fractions of trade with each country, times 100. Its upper limit is 100; the lower limit, assuming trade divided equally among 100 countries, would be 10, i.e. $\sqrt{\frac{100}{10{,}000}} \times 100$.

TABLE 9–1. *Geographic Concentration of Trade, about 1954*

Country	*Export Coefficient*	*Import Coefficient*	*Export Coefficient* / *Import Coefficient*
Panama	95.5	67.0	1.43
Eire	89.7	56.7	1.58
Colombia	79.8	64.2	1.24
Honduras	78.0	69.4	1.12
Mauritius	77.6	46.5	1.67
Nigeria	74.0	51.3	1.44
Mexico	73.7	81.2	0.91
Canada	63.9	74.9	0.85
Costa Rica	62.4	60.4	1.03
Rhodesia and Nyasaland	58.4	55.5	1.05
Trinidad and Tobago	50.0	47.5	1.05
Gold Coast	47.9	50.5	0.95
Burma	47.6	39.6	1.20
Thailand	43.5	35.7	1.22
Denmark	41.8	37.0	1.13
Brazil	41.5	37.4	1.11
Australia	41.2	49.5	0.83
Tanganyika	39.5	47.2	0.84
Indonesia	38.3	31.4	1.22
Greece	34.1	31.1	1.10
Finland	34.0	26.8	1.27
Netherlands Antilles	33.6	79.7	0.42
Argentina	32.1	26.8	1.20
Austria	31.8	39.7	0.80
Yugoslavia	31.3	37.0	0.85
Spain	29.5	28.4	1.04
Belgium-Luxembourg	29.4	28.6	1.03
Turkey	29.3	28.4	1.03
Iceland	29.1	30.8	0.95
Sweden	28.4	30.4	0.93
Norway	28.0	25.9	1.08
Hong Kong	27.6	30.0	0.92
United States	27.5	27.6	0.99
Portugal	27.4	28.0	0.98
Netherlands	27.0	29.6	0.91
Malaya and Singapore	26.0	38.2	0.68
Egypt	26.0	26.0	1.00
Japan	24.0	38.1	0.63
France	21.8	20.4	1.07
Italy	21.1	24.2	0.87
Western Germany	21.0	20.8	1.01
United Kingdom	18.7	19.4	0.96

Source: M. Michaely, "Concentration of Exports and Imports," *Economic Journal, 68* (1958), 732.

siderable opportunities for exploitation of monopsonistic advantage today, as Hirschman's table also did in 1938 when it was compiled.[8] But it does not follow that advantage has been taken of them, except by accident.

Hirschman's work attracted considerable interest as a quantitative approach to the links between international economics and international politics. Michael Michaely went further, however, and investigated the extent to which countries specialize by commodities in both exports and imports, to furnish an indication of the possibility of exerting monopoly or monopsony power in selected markets. In particular he wished to test the classical assumption, set forth by Mill, Marshall, and Taussig, that countries tend to specialize more in what they export than in what they import. This presumption was in fact supported by Michaely's findings, set forth in Table 9–2. In a separate article, the same author measures weighted shares in world trade by comparing not the value of a country's trade in relation to world trade, but the ratio of the value of its trade to total trade in the commodities it buys and sells, to gain still another—and more subtle—impression of its monopoly power in trade.[9]

Tariffs are also used discriminately between raw materials and finished products to affect the location of the higher forms of manufacture. A "tariff factory" may be attracted to a country by taxing imports of the finished product while admitting materials free. But two can play that game, and the exporting country can tax the export of raw materials while imposing no tariff on, or even subsidizing, the finished

8. For a high percentage of trade with a given country really to imply the possibility of exploitation, it must be assumed that the importing country depends upon the particular supply, and that the supply curve is relatively inelastic in the exporter.

9. M. Michaely, "The Shares of Countries in World Trade," *Review of Economics and Statistics*, *42* (1960), 307–17.

TABLE 9–2. *Commodity Concentration in Foreign Trade, about 1954*

Country	*Export Coefficient*	*Import Coefficient*	*Export Coefficient / Import Coefficient*
Mauritius	98.8	28.6	3.46
Netherlands Antilles	93.7	83.0	1.13
Egypt	84.2	18.6	4.54
Colombia	84.0	23.9	3.51
Gold Coast	83.5	21.4	3.89
Iceland	80.3	19.1	4.21
Burma	74.4	24.2	3.08
Trinidad and Tobago	72.7	30.5	2.39
Thailand	68.3	21.4	3.19
Honduras	65.0	19.7	3.30
Panama	62.8	16.8	3.74
Costa Rica	60.5	18.8	3.21
Australia	50.8	27.0	1.88
Malaya and Singapore	49.8	25.4	1.96
Nigeria	49.3	24.3	2.03
Kenya-Uganda	49.0	22.9	2.14
Greece	46.2	19.3	2.40
Tanganyika	44.6	22.8	1.95
Indonesia	41.7	24.5	1.70
Turkey	39.7	23.5	1.69
Eire	38.3	16.5	2.31
Finland	38.1	19.2	1.98
Mexico	35.0	26.8	1.30
Libya	34.1	18.9	1.80
Spain	33.9	24.5	1.39
Rhodesia and Nyasaland	32.5	20.2	1.61
Argentina	30.6	21.5	1.42
Sweden	28.1	18.5	1.52
Austria	27.7	19.7	1.41
Denmark	27.1	18.5	1.46
Belgium-Luxembourg	25.5	15.5	1.65
Norway	25.5	23.4	1.09
Canada	24.9	18.0	1.38
Japan	24.8	26.4	0.94
Portugal	24.7	19.1	1.30
Western Germany	22.3	15.6	1.43
Yugoslavia	21.4	26.1	0.82
Hong Kong	20.6	16.0	1.28
Italy	20.5	20.7	0.99
United Kingdom	19.2	16.1	1.19
United States	18.8	20.5	0.92
France	18.0	20.4	0.88
Netherlands	16.9	16.0	1.06

Source: M. Michaely, "Concentration of Exports and Imports," p. 725.

export. The result is a form of dueling. In the paper industry in Europe, where the contest has been particularly widespread between the producers of wood in Scandinavia and the consumers of paper on the Continent, the producers have gradually been gaining because of the limited supply of wood.

The infant-industry argument applies both at the national and at the international level. If there are really substantial economies to scale, the whole world benefits from a tariff that enables an industry to expand along its long-run declining cost curve. When the process has been completed, the tariff is no longer needed. Some economists believe that the infant-industry argument applies not only to particular industries but to whole sectors, like manufacturing, which yield economies of agglomeration and training not found in the production of raw materials or foodstuffs. If this be so, it may be desirable to accept a lower current income through less effective resource allocation in the short run in order to grow at a faster rate. The argument will be touched upon again in Chapter 12.

TARIFFS, QUOTAS, AND MULTIPLE-EXCHANGE RATES AS SECOND-BEST POLICIES

Under ideal conditions free trade produces an efficiency optimum and a welfare maximum. But it does not follow that in circumstances short of the ideal every move toward free trade is a move in the direction of these goals. It may be a second-best policy to impose tariffs or quotas or even multiple-exchange rates to improve efficiency and to redistribute income between or within countries more in accordance with agreed ethical standards. Or such departures away or further away from free trade may be a third-best or a fourth-best or a tenth-best policy, superior to the alternatives, if less satisfactory than the impractical policies closer to the ideal.

In depression brought about by a decline in domestic investment, for example, the optimal solution is to restore domestic investment. Failing this, there is a case for other domestic spending, such as by the government. As a worst positive course, recognized as a "beggar-thy-neighbor" policy, a country can seek to export its unemployment by stimulating exports or reducing imports, thereby diverting income previously spent on imports to domestic producers. Even this policy may be better than inaction.

The same reasoning applies to other types of difficulties. Suppose a deficit in the balance of payments develops because of a decline in demand abroad for an important export. The orthodox prescription is to reallocate the resources no longer needed for the old export good into incremental exports or import-competing industries by means of the price mechanism—either through the unassisted price mechanism, working with constant or slightly reduced national money income, or, if the effect needed is sizable, with the assistance of currency depreciation. But if the price system works only slowly, or if depreciation has to be ruled out because of recent experience with inflation that has left the public identifying depreciation with inflation and ready to undertake destabilizing speculation and capital flight at the first sign of either, government may feel obliged to apply tariffs, exchange control, and quantitative restrictions. This results in what Galbraith has called the disequilibrium system, with the market cleared not by price but by restrictions on producers, consumers, or both.[10]

Under extreme pathological conditions of this sort—in-

10. J. K. Galbraith, "The Disequilibrium System," *American Economic Review*, 37 (1947), 287–302.

effectively controlled inflation, overvalued exchange rates—it will be necessary to restrain imports which are cheap, push exports which are unprofitable, and prevent capital flight which offers safety. Such a system, working against the incentives of the price system, is likely to be effective only in the short run. Price control and rationing, which are the domestic equivalent of the disequilibrium system, are generally operable in wartime, under the incentive of patriotism. They may even function effectively (though this is debatable) in a postwar recovery program of limited duration. The question is an open one, however, whether the disequilibrium system—rationing and price controls internally, and overvaluation, import restrictions, export set-asides, and control of capital movements on the international front—can be made to work efficiently over the longer pull involved, say, in a program of economic development.

There can be no doubt that the incentives under this system are wrong. Profits from importing are enormous, if one can get a license. Foreign capital equipment looks cheap, relative to the domestic high cost of labor. Exporting is a poor bet, since it involves selling at low prices what was produced at inflationary cost. A country like Israel with strong patriotism may be able to operate the system for a time. But not for long.

One version of the disequilibrium system is the multiple-exchange rate, in which different rates are charged and paid for foreign exchange used and earned for different purposes. Where the overvalued rate cuts out a marginal export, a lower rate can be allowed, while the higher rate helps extract from the world, on an export which enjoys a special position in world demand, a monopoly price. In imports, necessities are bought cheaply at overvalued rates, but the temptation to import other products, including luxuries, is restrained by requiring them to be bought only at a depreciated rate. The multiple-exchange-rate system relieves some of the pressure of disequilibrium by allowing ultimate satisfaction at a market-clearing price. This converts the problem of surveillance into one of ensuring that prime exports do not receive the high rate for exports, and low-priority imports do not obtain cheap exchange. The distortion of incentives remains, and equal or stronger governmental pressure must be exerted to contain it.

REGIONAL DISCRIMINATION

Government interference with trade frequently follows regional lines. In his pioneering studies for the League of Nations on the multilateral clearing mechanism in world payments, Folke Hilgerdt found a substantial increase in bilateral balancing between regions between 1928 and 1938, as one country after another cut down imports, especially from those countries with which it had large import surpluses.[11] The figures are shown in absolute amounts in Table 9–3, but reductions also took place in percentage terms, as the decline in multilateral trade outstripped that in total trade. The balances in the matrix will differ depending on whether one measures them in the exporting or the importing country. This difference is due, of course, to the fact that the value of imports is higher than that of exports, by the value of freight, insurance, and so on, as well as to the inaccuracy of trade statistics, which fail to match on a country-by-country basis.

The decline in multilateral balancing was of course due to the Depression. Noncontinental Europe (Britain) actually enlarged its import surplus with Areas of Recent Settlement

11. League of Nations (F. Hilgerdt), *The Network of World Trade* (Geneva, 1942).

TABLE 9–3. *The Decline in Multilateral Trading, 1928–1938*
[*Interregional Balances of Exports over Imports (+), or Imports over Exports (−)*]
(in millions of dollars)

Trade of	*Tropics*		*United States*		*Areas of Recent Settlement*		*Continental Europe*		*Noncontinental Europe*		*Rest of World*	
With	*1928*	*1938*	*1928*	*1938*	*1928*	*1938*	*1928*	*1938*	*1928*	*1938*	*1928*	*1938*
Tropics	−100	+10	−950	−280	−130	−170	−690	−530	+190	−270	−260	−90
United States	+640	+70	—	—	−690	−420	−890	−440	−680	−470	−30	−260
Areas of Recent Settlement	+30	+40	+600	+340	−20	−20	−960	−330	−290	−490	−140	−50
Continental Europe	+340	+90	+620	+250	+710	+120	−290	−250	−900	−580	−120	−70
Noncontinental Europe	−300	+60	+610	+440	+170	+270	+670	+390	−10	−10	+10	+90
Rest of World	+130	−10	−130	+170	+100	−30	−30	−90	−80	−140	—	—
Total	+740	+260	+750	+920	+140	−250	−2,190	−1,250	−1,770	−1,960	−540	−380

Source: League of Nations (F. Hilgerdt), *The Network of World Trade,* tables 44, p. 77, and 48, p. 90.

(largely the Dominions). Clearing agreements designed to breach exchange controls had a bias in favor of neighbors. All these sorts of discrimination were to be reduced or eliminated by the rules of trading put forward by the United States during and after World War II, in Article VII of the Lend-Lease Act, the United Nations Charter, the lend-lease settlements, the Anglo-American Financial Agreement, the draft charter of the International Trade Organization, the General Agreement on Tariffs and Trade. But the "dollar shortage" intervened. Ragnar Frisch, the Norwegian economist, demonstrated that under certain circumstances discrimination involved less reduction in foreign trade than non-discrimination: countries that lacked dollars to trade with the United States should at least trade with one another.[12]

The rules would have led to a gradual elimination of discrimination as the dollar shortage eased and then became cured, had it not been for two provisions in them, agreed to by all: one provision permitted discrimination in certain products in trade among developing countries, on the ground that if a country lacked sufficient market to start an industry by itself, it could perhaps do so with protection from developed countries and access without hindrance to the market of other developing countries; the other provision permitted the existence of customs unions or free-trade areas, the establishment of which was to be approached gradually, if the participants wanted, but only if the firm intention existed of going all the way: 99 per cent discrimination was not allowed; 100 per cent was. Customs unions have been projected in Europe among six countries on the Continent; a free-trade area among the seven countries on the periphery (the United Kingdom, Norway, Sweden, Denmark, Austria, Switzerland, and Portugal); customs unions among five coun-

12. "On the Need for Forecasting a Multilateral Balance of Payments," *American Economic Review*, 37 (1947), 535–51.

tries in Central America (Nicaragua, Honduras, El Salvador, Guatemala, and Costa Rica); and in Latin America among Argentina, Brazil, Chile, Mexico, Paraguay, Peru, and Uruguay. Attempts to form a customs union have been in train for some years in the Arab League; and there is a strong possibility that one or more customs unions will be formed among the former African colonies gaining their independence in the last and approaching several years.

Erik Thorbecke has argued that increased regional trading has taken place within continental Europe and within the sterling and dollar areas for geographic, political, economic, and monetary reasons.[13] The geographic reasons are illustrated by the movement of Venezuelan oil more exclusively to the United States as a result of Europe's being supplied by the Middle East. This is not persuasive. Some Middle East oil moves to the United States, and United States coal goes for the first time to Europe. The political and economic reasons are significant. Europe seeks a new solidarity. So do the underdeveloped parts of the world as they work for economic development. Intra-European trade has risen faster than European trade with the outside world. (See Table 2–6.) This result was achieved before discriminatory tariff reduction had made much headway, and was the consequence both of the rapid rise in income and of the shifting of attention of European firms to opportunities in neighboring markets. Underdeveloped countries have much less mutual trade—in 1958, twenty Latin American countries and twelve Arab states had average imports within the group of 9.5 and 11.6 per cent respectively, as contrasted with 13 per cent for the European Free Trade Area (the Seven), and 32 per cent for the European Economic Community (the Six).

Within the sterling area, trade ties are linked to finance

13. *The Tendency towards Regionalization in International Trade, 1928–1956* (The Hague, Martinus Nijhoff, 1959).

and investment, which follow political lines. During the Depression but especially after the war, the United Kingdom forbade the export of capital except to the Commonwealth, and this had the effect of deepening trade channels, as noted in Table 2–3. The Commonwealth capital movement, at a time when Britain was short of capital, was criticized currently as wasteful, especially as some of the investments undertaken were of limited social value. Now the question is whether the close ties with the Commonwealth inhibit Britain from joining the fast growing and dynamic European Common Market, and if so, whether they are a help or a hindrance.

In the United States, the position of a favored trading partner is occupied by Canada.[14] Here considerations of geography, politics, economics, and finance all play a part. It may be said, indeed, that the locational factors in North America basically favor north-south rather than east-west economic integration—a subject reserved for discussion to Chapter 15. But despite lack of a customs union, in fact in spite of tariff policies which have protected Canadian manufacturing against the more powerful United States industry, and United States farmers and miners against low-cost competition from the north, trade flourishes without discrimination.

14. In terms of exports per dollar of the customers' national income, the United States' best customer is Mexico. In *An Essay on Trade and Transformation,* Burenstam Linder has calculated average propensities to import of thirty-two countries from each other, per thousand dollars of income per capita. Only nine figures are over 100 (10 per cent): Tunis from France, 222; Mexico from the United States, 160; Ghana from Britain, 157; New Zealand from Britain, 135; Canada from the United States, 132; Chile from the United States, 121; Austria from Germany, 119; Israel from the United States, 110; the Union of South Africa from Britain, 102.

10 INTERNATIONAL TRADE UNDER SOCIALISM

SOCIALISM IN ONE COUNTRY

In economic affairs as in so many other respects, it is difficult to disentangle in the experience of the Soviet Union what is Russian from what is socialistic. In 1913, Russian exports amounted to something like 7 to 12 per cent of national income. After virtually no trade in the early 1920s, they reached approximately 3.5 per cent at the interwar peak in 1931.[1] In 1959 the proportion was between 2.6 and 2.9 per cent.[2] One is tempted to ascribe the change to design: the Soviet policy of "planned proportionate development" was to build heavy industry, if necessary with imports, in

1. F. D. Holzman, "International Trade and Economic Growth: The Soviet Union (1917–1957) and the United States (1869–1913)," unpublished paper for the Social Science Research Council Conference, Princeton, May 1961.

2. See Note to Table 2–1.

order to free itself of dependence on outside sources of supply. The purpose of foreign trade was to obtain imports to make foreign trade ultimately unnecessary. But much of the relative decline in foreign trade can be explained by the natural evolution of a continent-size country: the ratio of exports to national income in the United States declined from 7.5 per cent in 1913 to 4 per cent in 1958, during part of which time the government was trying to liberalize trade policy. In addition, special features of Russian experience worked to reduce trade directly: as a result of the war the country experienced substantial territorial losses in regions with a high proportion of exports; 1913 imports had been financed in substantial part by bonds sold in Western Europe, especially France, whereas very few credits were available after the war; exports of agricultural products, stimulated prior to 1913 by the marketings of peasants anxious to get cash to buy land, were cut by agricultural reform in the early period, and not aided by the subsequent collectivization; finally, income distribution had been highly skewed in Tsarist Russia, favoring substantial imports of luxury consumption goods.

While these special Russian features played a part in the reduction of trade under the Communists, there can be no doubt of the influence of the longer-run antipathy to trade of a single socialist country of continental size in a hostile world. Imports, particularly of machinery and critically short materials, were vital. They were paid for by exports of wheat and timber, reduced in volume from before the war, and by somewhat expanded sales of petroleum, furs, and coal, plus sales of gold, and some limited credits.

The First Five-Year Plan called for a rapid expansion of trade as a step toward its elimination. Exports and imports both rose to a peak in 1931 before the full impact of the world economic crisis was felt. The proportion of consumption goods in imports was cut from 27 per cent in 1913 to 12 per cent in 1929 and 5 per cent in 1931. (See Table 10–4.) When during the Depression the terms of trade turned against it, the Soviet Union continued to export wheat, driving down the world price to 50 cents a bushel, at great cost in the starvation of masses of the Russian populace. This was not an effort to destroy the capitalist system, but an attempt to maintain equipment imports and to service outstanding loans. The experience was painful. Under the Second Five-Year Plan, and thereafter to the Second World War, foreign trade was reduced in the short run.

THE ORGANIZATION OF FOREIGN TRADE

Responsibility for the conduct of foreign trade in the Soviet Union has been divided between the Ministry of Foreign Trade, which produces the "foreign trade plan" with the foreign trade department of the Gosplan and concludes overall trade agreements, and a number of foreign trade corporations, largely specialized by commodities, whose functions are to deal with the Soviet producing and consuming enterprises and to negotiate specific contracts for purchases and sales abroad. The task of both units is the same as that of any other economic enterprise in the Soviet Union —to fulfill the plan and to make profits.

Whether foreign trade is profitable to the Soviet Union is difficult to calculate, both for the foreign observer and the Soviet planner. In the first place, the picture is confused by the overvaluation of the ruble. Soviet trade has been conducted largely in terms of foreign prices and foreign currencies. The ruble value of exports and imports is therefore inconsequential. The revaluations of 1936 and 1950, for example, occurred for reasons of internal monetary reform, and with them the ruble value of exports and imports was calculated anew in the historical record.[3] Overvaluation meant that all domestic operations appear to have been conducted at a loss, measured in domestic ruble prices and the nominal exchange rate, while imports make large paper profits on their sales to state enterprises. These profits, called "tariffs," are transferred to the state budget, from which apparent losses of the export organizations are made up.

This overvaluation is troublesome but not important, as long as the authorities are willing to come out even rather than try to make a profit. If Soviet relative prices reflect real relative scarcities, the profitability of Soviet trade could be calculated after balancing exports and imports and netting losses on the former with profits on the latter. There would be in fact no need to use the actual prices at which goods are transferred within the country, if these departed from real relative scarcities. It would suffice to use imaginary or "shadow prices" limited to foreign trade, provided that they reflected scarcity.

But planning in the Soviet Union has not proceeded on the basis of price calculations. The "law of proportionate planned development" proceeded by means of "materials balances," in which attention was given to requirements and what could physically be produced, with little attention to cost. In such a system, foreign trade could be ignored (autarky), or it could be used to correct for shortages resulting from delays in filling needs, and for surpluses resulting from random departures from plan fulfillment without regard to the relative costs and benefits of employing labor and capital

3. F. D. Holzman, "Some Financial Aspects of Soviet Foreign Trade," Joint Economic Committee, *Comparisons of the United States and Soviet Economies*, pt. II (Washington, G.P.O., 1959).

in export and import-competing industry.[4] The latter is in fact what has been done. Only after World War II, with the need to deal systematically with foreign trade because of the existence of socialism in more than one country, has attention been paid to the profitability of foreign trade.

The planning system used in the Soviet Union, moreover, was biased in directions that distorted the structure of foreign trade from what it might have been under shadow pricing. One bias had a theological basis: the devotion to the Marxist labor theory of value which ignores the productivity of capital and land. This tended to make capital-intensive and land-intensive goods cheaper than they would have been under a "competitive" system, to favor their export, and to favor imports of labor-intensive goods. Another was the strong state preference for capital formation, and penalization of consumption, which led to the imposition of much higher "tariffs" on consumer goods than on capital equipment and materials. Profit maximization would have favored more imports of consumer goods. A third bias was the pressure for plan fulfillment under planning which diverted potential exports to the domestic economy and applied pressure to make good production shortfalls. Strong counterpressures have been built into the system to prevent this bias from leading to bigger deficits than could be financed.

Another bias has been political in origin: a readiness to buy fish when Iceland was unable to sell its catch to the West, or to absorb Egyptian cotton, Cuban sugar, and similar surpluses elsewhere when there was a political advantage to be gained from it, without initially questioning whether the commodities would readily fit into domestic requirements or could be resold elsewhere at a profit or a tolerable

4. Charles Bettelheim, *Studies in the Theory of Planning* (Bombay and New York, Asia Publishing House, 1959), p. 251.

small loss. This same political bias has frequently been suspected in the dumping of exports—wheat in the 1930s, platinum, tin, aluminum, benzene, petroleum products after World War II.[5] A more satisfactory explanation has always been the Soviet need for foreign exchange, and the chance surpluses resulting from trade or overproduction.[6]

When it was alone in the interwar period as a socialist country, the Soviet Union operated its foreign trade on the whole without systematic rational calculus. Import needs consisted mainly of equipment and industrial materials which could not then be produced at home.[7] Exports were traditional items. To the extent that any rationale could be found for the system, it accorded to absolute advantage, and on the basis of vent-for-surplus.

SOCIALISM IN MANY COUNTRIES

The initial reaction of the Soviet Union to its dominant position in Eastern Europe after World War II was to grab anything and everything that was loose. From former Axis partners—Bulgaria, Hungary, Romania—stiff reparations

5. See the speech of Nelson A. Rockefeller in which he characterized Russian sales in 1958 as a "deliberate attempt to disrupt the market": *New York Times* (October 9, 1959), p. 14.

6. Alec Nove, "Soviet Trade and Soviet Aid," *Lloyds Bank Review*, n.s., *51* (1959), 11.

7. Holzman, "International Trade and Economic Growth," Table II–14, shows the percentage of requirements covered by imports in a number of lines. This percentage declines in virtually all lines, and frequently, as in lead, tin, nickel, aluminum, automobiles, from 100 per cent in 1909–13 to zero or less than 5 per cent in the second half of the 1950s. Only in zinc (100 per cent in 1913 to 18 per cent in 1955) and wool (26 per cent to 16 per cent) do substantial amounts of the items of consumption listed remain provided from abroad. The table does not cover tropical products, however, like coffee, tea, and cocoa.

were exacted, fixed in dollar amounts, but specified in commodities valued at 1938 prices. Exploitation in Eastern Germany was more direct. Large quantities of machinery were stripped from some factories and shipped back to the Soviet Union. Other plants were acquired in place, and as late as 1954 were operating for the benefit of the Soviet military administration. Poland, a former ally, was subjected to less direct exploitation. In return for 15 per cent of German reparations to the U.S.S.R., Poland undertook to deliver large quantities of coal to the Soviet Union, again at prices favoring the customer. Quarrels over whether joint Soviet-Yugoslav companies in the latter country favored the Soviet Union contributed to the break between the two countries.

By 1949 this position had changed. Czechoslovakia had been added to the Eastern bloc. Trade policies increasingly had to include the new Asian member, Communist China. As the Cold War settled in, the Soviet Union was more and more forced to be concerned with the welfare of its satellites. The Marshall Plan provided a Western challenge that could not be ignored. The Soviet Union extended credits to its satellites and adjusted reparation burdens. In January 1949 a Council for Mutual Economic Assistance (C.E.M.A.) was established at Moscow to expand intrabloc trade and to assist in the coordination of national economic plans.

C.E.M.A. achieved very little while Stalin was alive. Bilateral trade agreements were negotiated among its member countries. Each country of the bloc, however, continued to follow mainly the "law of proportionate Socialist development," as it aped Soviet interwar policies and stressed the priority of the capital-goods sector. Trade grew gradually, and some specialization of production was achieved in machinery. Some "industrial treaties" were negotiated among the satellites—though not with the Soviet Union—in which each country agreed not to produce certain articles available in the other. But broadly speaking, parallel expansion of the capital-goods sector in the Soviet bloc threatened to result in excess capacity in machinery and equipment, and put great pressure on fuel and on raw materials supply. Both these tendencies have persisted, despite efforts to eliminate them. Slowly it was recognized that the existence of a number of socialist countries instead of one furnished a basis for long-term specialization and exchange, rather than autarky.[8]

Stalin's death in March 1953 was followed by the "New Course" in economic policy, curtailing investment and favoring consumption, both in the Soviet Union and in Eastern European countries. The new emphasis on consumption can be seen in Table 10–1, showing the percentage composition of the Soviet Union's exports and imports, on somewhat different bases first from 1913 to 1938 and then from 1938

8. *Extracts from China Mainland Magazines,* U.S. Department of State, Consulate-General, Hong Kong, Dec. 23, 1957 (No. 122), quoted by C. A. Frost in a thesis "The Economic Development of Communist China" (Fletcher School of Law and Diplomacy, unpublished):

> The international environment in which we now find ourselves is different from that in which the Soviet Union found itself when building socialism. The Soviet Union, and in particular, the People's Democracies of East Europe generally speaking have a great capacity of machine-building industry and hope to supply our country with more machines. From the standpoint of international cooperation between socialist countries, it would appear that our country can produce less machines for the time being and solve our problem through international cooperation and concentrate more construction on projects which are more essential.

In the following year, however, a Chinese writing in a Soviet economic journal tried to have it both ways: "The creation in Communist China of an integrated industrial system will not lead to a weakening of its ties with other countries of the socialist camp. . . . Division of labor and specialization by products within these countries in correspondence with their economic possibilities and natural resources will receive further development." *Voprosi Ekonomiki* (Problems of Economics), *1* (1958), 17.

TABLE 10–1. *The Structure of Soviet Foreign Trade, 1913–1958 (percentage breakdown by broad commodity classes)*

1913–1938

	Exports				*Imports*			
Class	*1913*	*1929*	*1932*	*1938*	*1913*	*1929*	*1932*	*1938*
Animals	2.3	0.3	0.0	0.0	1.3	1.4	2.6	3.8
Foodstuffs	57.7	21.2	22.5	30.5	17.3	8.4	7.5	9.0
Raw materials and semimanufactures	34.4	62.7	53.5	50.4	48.6	43.6	16.5	39.6
Manufactured goods	5.6	15.8	24.0	19.1	32.8	46.6	73.4	47.6

Source: Alexander Baykov, *Soviet Foreign Trade* (Princeton, Princeton University Press, 1946), appendix table III.

1938–1958

	Exports				*Imports*			
Class	*1938*	*1950*	*1955*	*1958*	*1938*	*1950*	*1955*	*1958*
Machinery and equipment	5.0	11.8	17.5	18.5	34.5	21.5	30.2	24.5
Fuel and raw materials	57.7	64.4	67.9	65.9	60.7	63.3	51.5	51.6
Oil and oil products	7.8	2.4	6.7	10.0				
Timber products	20.1	2.4	4.0	4.6				
Ores and concentrates					2.6	5.8	8.2	9.3
Metals					25.9	7.2	6.7	7.3
Grain	21.3	12.1	8.3	8.3				
Consumers' goods	16.0	11.7	6.3	7.3	4.8	15.8	18.3	23.9

Source: A. Nove and D. Donnelly, *Trade with Communist Countries* (London, Macmillan, 1960), pp. 92–93.

to 1958. This relaxation intensified the foreign trade problem, by underlining the excess capacity in machinery, and reducing the agricultural surpluses available for export. Moreover, beginning about 1953, the early Soviet reconstruction loans to the Eastern satellites began falling due.

In the face of these difficulties, a new effort was made to

address the problem of coordinating national plans and trading multilaterally. In March 1954 a full plenary session of the C.E.M.A. met for the first time since 1950 and recommended measures for reducing parallel investments, much along the lines of the "industrial treaties." Another plenary session in May 1954 stressed the necessity for coordinating plans, but without evident result. Bloc trade continued to stagnate. It was not until May 1956, in the seventh plenary session, that broad lines of specialization were defined for each C.E.M.A. member, and suggestions issued for the distribution of production of 600 types of industrial machinery and equipment. Twelve permanent commissions were created for various industrial sectors. Materials balances for the entire bloc were constructed to serve as a basis for coordinating investment in the most important products in the 1956–60 Five-Year Plan just then getting under way. Long-term agreements based on these balances, however, had to be held up pending the adjustment of various plans.[9] In particular the Soviet Union, which had greatly expanded its proportion of trade within the Eastern bloc to total trade, as Table 10–2 shows, put pressure on the satellites to depend on it more for machinery and less for raw materials.

With the East German uprising and the Hungarian Revolution in October 1956, these last decisions had to be modified. Too much pressure had been applied to the standards of living of the Eastern satellites. New Soviet credits were

9. Note the possibilities of conflict which can be resolved only on an arbitrary basis in the absence of an adequate international system of prices. Czech exports of shoe-making machinery to Bulgaria were opposed by Hungarian and Polish exporters of shoes. This question, it was said, had to be resolved on the highest planning [political?] level. (Remark of a Czech foreign trade expert, UNESCO conference on East-West Trade, Prague, December 1960.)

extended, and foodstuffs supplied from east to west. The Soviet Union also increased its purchases of the output of Eastern European industries suffering from excess capacity.

TABLE 10–2. *Intra-Eastern Bloc Trade, as a Percentage of Total Trade, for Selected Years, 1938–1957*

	1938		*1948*		*1957*	
	Exports	*Imports*	*Exports*	*Imports*	*Exports*	*Imports*
U.S.S.R.	7	6	40	45	66	65
Eastern European satellites[a]	14	16	31	43	63	67
China	0	2	0	0	62	65

[a]Bulgaria, Czechoslovakia, Hungary, Poland, and Romania, but not including Eastern Germany or Yugoslavia.

Source: Computed from United Nations, *Direction of International Trade, 1959.*

These short-run measures were intended to be supplemented by more far-reaching change. It was agreed in principle to widen international specialization and exchange, and to coordinate fifteen-year plans for the 1960–75 period. Trade was to be extended to manufactured consumers' goods and to foodstuffs. The only remaining question was how to do it. In December 1958 an agreement was announced on specialization in plastics, chemical staple fiber, and synthetic fiber. A month later, at the twenty-first meeting of the Communist party, Premier Khrushchev pronounced his blessing on the international division of labor among socialist countries. Since that time the experts have been working to devise a rational system of multilateral specialization and trade among socialist countries. They are still working (March 1962). Meanwhile, trade proceeds on an empirical, bilateral, hit-or-miss basis.

If we believe what socialist writers say, trade among them is conducted in a planned way, in accordance with the laws of proportionality and proportional development, with respect for national sovereignty, noninterference in the affairs of other countries, friendship, and mutual aid. Such trade is said to take into account the various trading countries' needs and resources, to be based on scientific studies of rentability, and to serve to equalize incomes among trading partners. All this is said to be in sharp contrast with trade among free-enterprise economies, which exploits the weaker trading partner. Capitalist trade is discriminatory, monopolistic, and profit-making, in contrast to socialist trade, which is alleged to be equitable, based on mutual aid, and rentable. Socialist writers and speakers produce these expressions endlessly, and it is difficult to determine whether they think they mean anything by them. What is clear at close range, however, is that the present empirical basis of trading has proved less and less satisfactory, and the search is on for something that will allow eight countries to plan their production and trade simultaneously on an extended basis, with trade balanced multilaterally for each partner, at the same time leaving flexibility in the system for such contingencies as crop failures, industrial breakdowns, and changed demands or technology.

Under a Lange-Lerner system of socialist prices, it might be possible to carry out specialized production on a decentralized basis in which individual plants maximized "profits"—rather like the system being evolved by Yugoslavia. The latter is a replica of the free-market system, without its income distribution, leaving little room for long-run planning. Or planning might be done on a centralized basis with batteries of computers, if current prices represented not merely current values in social rather than private terms, but current social values discounted for future changes.[10] But where prices bear only a limited and distorted relationship to social values, it is far from clear how a rational basis for international specialization can be devised.[11] Many suggestions have been put forward in the literature of the Eastern bloc for basing bloc trade on comparative costs, but it is never clear how these are to be determined. Comparative labor productivities have been suggested, following on the labor theory of value, or land–labor ratios, or "profits" on exports and imports. They are theoretically invalid.

An important aspect of optimizing trade is to make it multilateral. Only by the most far-fetched coincidence would a series of countries achieve optimal specialization among themselves, and balanced trade for each country, with the separate trade of each pair also balanced bilaterally. There is an obvious need in the Eastern trade bloc, therefore, for a multilateral balancing system. It was a serious departure from efficiency for the Soviet Union to balance trade bilaterally in the interwar period, except for some use of sterling and dollars. The problem has been much more serious with socialism in many countries.

10. Along some such lines as those suggested by Ragnar Frisch in "Outline of a System of Multicompensatory Trade," *Review of Economics and Statistics, 30* (1948), 265–71.

11. See Hollis B. Chenery, "Comparative Advantage and Development Policy," *American Economic Review, 51* (1961), 42: "When the Soviet planning system was transplanted to the satellite countries, it ran into difficulties because of the inability to determine the advantages to be secured by trade. According to Balassa, the idea of comparative advantage did not exist in Hungarian development (at least until very recently) although trade had a high ratio to GNP. Exports are determined by import 'needs,' and the institutional structure is such as to encourage exporters to meet targets for exports without regard to production costs. Since prices do not reflect resource use, it is impossible to determine where comparative advantage lies and to what extent the trade pattern deviates from the optimum."

One possible solution is to settle bilateral imbalances within the bloc in foreign exchange, e.g. with sterling or dollars. But this would be unworthy of the dignity of socialism, and it would require running the risk of intervention. The Soviet Union does settle its import balance with Finland in sterling and gold needed by the latter in external bloc trade, but there is no evidence of regular use of foreign exchange otherwise. An obvious alternative is to settle bilateral imbalances in rubles. An agreement was signed in 1957 providing for multilateral settlements in rubles but never took effect. For it to work, a given amount of rubles must have more or less the same meaning for different countries, which implies some link between rubles and Soviet export prices. Until recently this has never been the case. The 1961 revaluation of the ruble may constitute a step in this direction.

Socialist apologists insist that trade in the Eastern bloc is nondiscriminatory, and an agreement signed in 1950 prohibits price discrimination in intrabloc trade. But the data suggest that each country does not charge the same price for the same good to all countries, but rather that the Soviet Union charges higher prices to the Communist bloc than to Western countries, and pays lower.[12] In theory, the Eastern bloc trades at world market prices, adjusted to eliminate the

12. Horst Mendershausen, "Terms of Trade between the Soviet Union and Smaller Communist Countries, 1955–1957," *Review of Economics and Statistics, 41* (1959), 106–18. Mendershausen's conclusion has been challenged by Holtzman, who maintains (in an unpublished paper) that all countries in the bloc trade at prices which are higher than prices in trade with the West for goods in which the bloc has a comparative disadvantage vis-à-vis the West (and lower for some articles in which the bloc has a comparative advantage). The first effect is similar to that of a customs union.

effects of cyclical or ephemeral changes.[13] In practice, of course, there is great difficulty in choosing the appropriate world price, not only on account of transport costs and discounts, but because of the lack of quoted prices on differentiated products. As exporters of compressors to the Soviet Union, the Czechs may quote a General Electric price in Schenectady, while the Soviet Union refers to a low Hitchi price in Japan. How the compromise comes out may be related to a parallel bargain on Russian sales of cotton to Czechoslovakia. In these circumstances it is impossible to measure exploitation in the bloc by comparing prices only between the West and the satellite trading partners. Double distortions may be offsetting in terms of exploitation, and go some distance to offsetting the bias of bilateralism. But the system is far from rational.

Socialist policy on international investment has also been slow to evolve. The subject has arisen in the bloc only recently, not in connection with equalizing incomes between countries, as socialist ideology assumes is done by trade, but with the need to increase the supply of short raw materials in an efficient manner. Historically, the Soviet Union made loans within the bloc only during the reconstruction period after 1948 and during the aftermath of the October 1956 uprisings. Now consideration is being given to international investment where capital can be more productive in one country than another.[14] This increases the need for prices that reflect scarcities and can be compared internationally.

13. For example, the Soviet Union has not reduced the price of oil charged in Eastern bloc trade to match the decline in world oil prices (especially after unquoted rebates and discounts) of the last two years. On the other hand, it did not raise its prices on raw materials during the Korean boom.

14. Such at least appears to be the meaning of statements like that of N. Silvianov, in "Novii Etap v Razvitii Mezhdunarodnovo Sotsialistlches-

EAST-WEST TRADE

East-West trade has grown absolutely, as shown in Table 10–3, though it has declined relative to the total trade of the Soviet Union, of China, and of Eastern Europe.[15] The table measures the trade of the Soviet Union from 1938 and 1948, but that of Eastern Europe only from 1948. Such trade rep-

TABLE 10–3. *East-West Trade, 1938–1957*
(outside Soviet-bloc trade with the world)
(in millions of dollars)

	1938		*1948*		*1955*		*1957*	
	Exports	*Imports*	*Exports*	*Imports*	*Exports*	*Imports*	*Exports*	*Impo*
Soviet Union	234	252	444	422	928	651	1,298	1,47
Eastern Europe[a]			963	930	1,490	1,525	1,694	1,46
China					426	110	568	24
Total (listed items)	234	252	1,407	1,352	2,844	2,286	3,560	3,19

[a]Including Eastern Germany but not Yugoslavia.

Source: United Nations, *Direction of International Trade, 1959.*

resents currently one-third of the trade of the Eastern bloc, but only one or two per cent of all trade of countries outside the bloc. The subject remains controversial. Western industrial countries, and especially the United States, have re-

---

kovo Razdelenie Truda" (New Stage in the Development of the International Socialist Division of Labor), *Voprosi Ekonomiki,* 2. (1959), 21: "All this means that methods have to be found to equalize conditions between countries with a structure of investment requiring more capital and those with less."

15. The percentage of Eastern trade carried on with the West is the difference between 100 per cent and the percentages set out in Table 10–2. Thus Soviet trade with the West has fallen from 55–60 per cent in 1948 to 35 per cent in 1957.

mained suspicious of Soviet and Chinese intentions, and attempted to limit exports to the Soviet Union of strategic materials and machinery that would increase Soviet war-making potential. The United States has banned all trade with Communist China. On the other side, the Soviet Union has claimed willingness to expand trade with non-Communist countries, while affirming its independence from the necessity for doing so. But trade has been circumscribed further by relative shortages in the Eastern bloc of goods of a kind marketable at satisfactory prices in the West. The Soviet Union and satellite countries want credits from the West, and offer in trade relatively simple, general-purpose machinery, not suited to Western industrial production methods, and redundant raw materials, such as petroleum. Exchanges of this sort of machinery, or complete factories, against primary products from underdeveloped countries, however, as discussed presently, may fit neatly the Eastern bloc's overcapacity in machinery lines and shortages of raw materials and consumers' goods.

While political factors and shortages have been important in holding East-West trade down to modest proportions, there is a long-run problem of conducting mutually advantageous intercourse between free markets and controlled economies. Let us leave aside the fact that trade cannot reach a world optimum because the socialist economy is distorted by bias from what it would have been under a competitive market or Lange-Lerner socialist system.[16] Some trade is

16. Europe incurred a large loss in gains from trade as a result of the reduction in Soviet exports of timber after World War II. This reduction was due partly to wartime destruction, partly to increased domestic demand from construction. It is probable that a rational calculus of social costs and benefits would have led the Soviet Union to take advantage of the high prices of timber in Europe and to invest in railroads for the sake of making more timber available to Baltic ports.

better than no trade. There will be gains for the free economy if it can sell dearer and buy cheaper from the socialist economy than it could under East-West autarky. The asymmetry between private trade on the one hand and the state on the other nevertheless poses several questions about the regulation and conduct of trade: What is really meant by nondiscrimination, or by an agreement to remove quantitative restrictions, or by a guarantee that only commercial considerations will govern trade? The intervention of the state automatically introduces monopoly elements. Moreover, while socialist theory claims that planning introduces stability, experience has shown that changes in both offers and requirements occur with great abruptness from one plan to the next, and much more sharply than changes in market economies, unstable though they be. Attempts to work out criteria by which to determine the presence of dumping in the General Agreement on Tariffs and Trade were met by the statement of Czechoslovakia, which along with Poland is a member, that different criteria were needed for socialist than for capitalist countries. No progress was made in developing such criteria, however, in the absence of information on production costs.

Several minor points concerning East-West trade merit mention. Western exports of complex manufactured goods are inhibited by the fact that the Soviet Union fails to respect Western patents, and copies technical improvements without payment of royalties. The Soviet Union also insists on arbitration within its jurisdiction, where the chances of a foreigner's winning a case against the government are exiguous. It has claimed diplomatic immunity and freedom from suit for its trading organizations abroad. On all these points, the Soviet Union will yield if forced to, but its pressure is continuous. On the other hand, the Soviet bloc has been upset by the nonfulfillment by the West of trade agreements, seemingly failing to understand that a Western state guarantee of the right to export or import, given to private enterprise, is not an obligation to trade. But while these economic and technical problems are real and difficult, they are not insoluble. "The missing ingredients in any negotiation with the Soviet bloc are less likely to be technical ingenuity than confidence and goodwill."[17]

It was noted earlier that there was probably little to the claim that the Soviet Union has attempted to disrupt capitalistic markets by dumping commodities. (Such attempts would in any case be easy to counter with a little ingenuity; it is hard to see how an effective economy can be undermined by gifts.) But the use of trade as a political weapon by the Soviet Union—purchasing a large proportion of a small country's total exports, and using the threat of trade cessation to influence domestic policies—is not excluded. The problem has already been posed—first in Iceland, then in Afghanistan and Finland, later in Ceylon, more recently in Egypt. It may arise for Cuba. The abrupt cancellation by the Soviet Union in 1958 of its credit agreements with Yugoslavia, and more recently the cessation of trade with Albania, show that the threat is not an empty one. Here is where the trading partners, and especially underdeveloped countries, need to show themselves sufficiently jealous of their independence to limit the danger.

17. Raymond Vernon, "Prospects and Policies in Trade with the Soviet Bloc," paper submitted to the Conference on Trade Policy held by the Committee for a National Trade Policy, Jan. 27–28, 1960, Washington, D.C.

SOCIALIST BLOC TRADE WITH UNDERDEVELOPED COUNTRIES

Within East-West trade an increasing proportion of the total has been between the Eastern bloc and the underdeveloped countries (i.e. the rest of the world except for the United States, Canada, Western Europe, Australia, New Zealand, and Japan), as shown in Table 10–4. This has been a

TABLE 10–4. *Eastern Bloc Trade with Underdeveloped Countries, as a Percentage of Total Trade, for Selected Years, 1938–1955*

	1938		*1948*		*1955*	
	Exports	*Imports*	*Exports*	*Imports*	*Exports*	*Imports*
Soviet Union	18	15	14	28	51	56
Eastern Europe[a]	14	14	16	16	40	33
Communist China	54	25	55	25	65	43
Total	22	17	25	21	49	45

[a]Not including Eastern Germany or Yugoslavia.

Source: United Nations, *Direction of International Trade, 1959.*

source of concern to Western industrial leaders, fearful of increasing political influence and subversion. Socialist bloc trade with and credits to underdeveloped countries are small by comparison with those of the United States, Western Europe and the British Dominions, but some observers, extrapolating the rapid increase which has taken place from 1950 to 1958, see the bloc as eventually a dominant trading power. Moreover, by focusing trade and loans on a limited group of countries within the total, the bloc can have considerable impact.

Up to the present, however, the growth of commercial relations of the Socialist bloc with the underdeveloped world is largely explicable on economic grounds. These relations consist basically of the exchange of Soviet bloc machinery and equipment in surplus against raw materials in short supply, the latter for immediate or delayed delivery. While the Soviet Union is itself a net importer of machinery and equipment vis-à-vis Eastern Europe, and the whole bloc seeks advanced machines from Western industrial countries, there remains room for the profitable export of mass-produced simple machinery to underdeveloped countries by the Soviet bloc.[18] This triangular trade is particularly suited to the needs of the industrial countries of Eastern Europe—Czechoslovakia and Eastern Germany, with their overcapacity in machinery and need for fuel and materials.

Not all Soviet bloc transactions are strictly economic. Burmese rice was imported in 1954 far in excess of domestic needs, and was re-exported (to Burma's displeasure). Imports of Cuban sugar square curiously with the position of the Soviet Union as a normal exporter of this commodity, and sugar is now a drug on the market in Eastern countries. The dramatic Soviet loans for the Aswan dam in Egypt and the Bhutai steel mill in India were also costly. But the majority of transactions have an economic basis, and fit, moreover, into the needs of underdeveloped countries, as well as those of the Eastern bloc. Later, when industrialization has made progress in such places as India, it will be interesting to see whether they will become restive, like Communist China, and unwilling to accept assignment in international specialization to labor-intensive, primary products, and want, in turn, to export machinery.

One Western fear is that the Soviet Union will use bilat-

18. It is not clear whether this trade would have been profitable starting from scratch, but once the investment in machinery plants has been made, and regarded as a sunk cost, it probably becomes so.

eral clearing methods to exploit the dependence of its trading partners, much as Germany did in Southeastern Europe in the 1930s. It is true that bilateral clearing methods are used, although increasingly the trade is becoming triangular among the underdeveloped countries, Eastern Europe, and the Soviet Union. But there is no evidence of attempts to build up large clearing deficits by the Soviet Union: most arrangements in fact call for initial Soviet credits to the underdeveloped countries. And where the trading partner insists, as India has done, the Soviet Union has even consented to keep accounts in convertible sterling.

Eastern European countries depend on foreign trade.[19] The Soviet Union and China, whose operations are much more feared, do not, to anything like the same extent. Moreover, there is no evidence that Soviet leaders give a high priority to foreign economic adventures. In the Twenty-First Congress of the Communist party and the plenary meeting of the Central Committee in June 1959, attention was focused almost wholly on economic issues, with scarcely any mention of foreign relations or foreign aid. Current planning does not envisage any radical increases in Soviet bloc trade with, or aid to, the underdeveloped world. The emphasis of the Soviet Union is on catching up with the West at home.

19. Foreign trade turnover per capita in 1958 for Eastern Europe was $115, as compared with $43 for the Soviet Union. These figures compare with $176 for the United States, $276 for the European Economic Community (the Six), and $293 for the rest of the O.E.E.C.

11 THE EFFECTS OF GROWTH ON TRADE

SYNTHESIS

The influence of growth on trade has not been entirely absent from the earlier discussion of factor endowments, technology, and capacity to transform. Dynamic aspects cannot be excluded in dealing with the static. It may, however, be useful to pull some of the dynamic elements together and to see what, if any, net results emerge from them.

Table 11–1 gives a schematic representation of the major influences at work to alter a country's foreign trade at various stages of its economic growth.[1] The schema is highly general as well as purely qualitative. At most stages of development some forces will be operating to expand trade; others to re-

1. Reproduced in slightly modified form from my *International Economics* (rev. ed. Homewood, Ill., 1958), p. 421.

TABLE 11–1. *Impact on Trade of Factors Conditioning Economic Growth*

Factors / Stage of Development	Resources (Land) (1)	Social Structure (Labor) (2)	Capital (3)	Technical Change (4)	Transformation (Capacity to Reallocate) (5)	Scale of Production (6)	Total Increases, Decreases Inc.	Dec.
Stagnation (a)	Fixed	Static	$I_d = S$ (both low) $X = M$ (both low)	Static	None; low supply elasticities; t of t matter of luck	Small (village)		
Commercial revolution (b)	Expansion (due to incorporation in market) $X\uparrow$	Beginnings of social mobility, money economy	$I_d = X$ (both low) $X = M$ (both $\uparrow$)	Once-for-all change (Myint) $X\uparrow$ (imitation) $M_c\uparrow$ (demonstration effect)	Elasticities expanding but low	Expansion at home; production for world market in enclaves	4	–
Economic growth (take-off) (c)	Discovery and technical change expand, resources $X\uparrow$	Development entrepreneurial class $S\uparrow$ increased income $M_c\uparrow$	$I_d\uparrow$, $I_d > S$ $M_p\uparrow M > X$ borrowing abroad	Technical change (imitation) $M_p\uparrow$	Resources mobile $X\uparrow \downarrow M\downarrow$ income rising $M\uparrow$	Integration of home and world markets $X\uparrow M\uparrow$ growth of M-competing industry $M\downarrow$	8	2
Maturity (d)	Discovery $X\uparrow$ Depletion $X\downarrow M\uparrow$	High income $S\uparrow$	$S > I_d$ $X > M$ lending abroad $X\uparrow$	Innovation new goods $X\uparrow M\downarrow$ new ways of producing old goods $X\uparrow M\downarrow$	Elasticities high, income rising, demand for services $M\uparrow$ absolutely $M\downarrow$ relatively	Product differentiation $X\uparrow M\downarrow$	7	5
Decline (e)	Depletion $X\downarrow M\uparrow$	Fair shares S reduced social mobility; demonstration effect $C\uparrow$	$I_d > S$ $M > X$ using up foreign assets	Slowing down of technical change, imitation abroad $X\downarrow$; imitation of foreign innovation $M\uparrow$	Elasticities declining, allocation below optimal t of $t\downarrow$	Declining scale as markets are reduced through protection $M\downarrow$	2	3

C consumption
I investment
I_d domestic investment
S savings
X exports
M imports
M_c imports of consumption goods
M_p imports of producers goods
t of t terms of trade
$\uparrow$ increase
$\downarrow$ decrease
$>$ is greater than
$<$ is less than

strict it. We are, of course, not interested in the impact on the balance of payments, or the relative impact on exports *(X)* and imports *(M)*. The right-hand column suggests, however, that in the early stages of growth, particularly the commercial revolution, trade tends to expand. But as the process continues, there is a variety of conflicting tendencies, with the balance shifting from expansion to relative contraction.

THE LAW OF DECLINING TRADE

This schematic presentation supports, in a very general way, the view that after an initial expansion, foreign trade tends to decline relative to total economic activity. This tendency has been hypothesized directly by Werner Sombart, the German economic historian, who formulated a law of the declining importance of foreign trade. A recent attempt has been made to test whether this is in fact the case, and if so to explore the reasons.[2] Table 11–2 and Figure 11–1 present data from this study, and from one by Rolf R. Piekars[3] for some other countries. They provide a very general support for the validity of the law.

But the support is only general. In fact, Kuznets believes that "there is no prevalence of trends in one direction."[4] Deutsch and Eckstein are aware that there are numerous exceptions to the tendency, but believe that on a weighted basis, from 1913 to 1957, the existence of the law is established. Trade has a way of starting to decline, and then ris-

2. K. W. Deutsch and A. Eckstein, "National Industrialization and the Declining Share of the International Economic Sector, 1890–1959," *World Politics, 13* (1961), 267–99.

3. "Proportion of Foreign Trade in National Product and Economic Growth" (doctoral dissertation, Johns Hopkins, 1958), cited by Simon Kuznets in *Economic Growth,* pp. 101–03.

4. *Economic Growth,* p. 100.

TABLE 11–2. *Ratio of Foreign Trade to National Income, for Selected Countries, 1799–1959*
(average of exports and imports to national income or to income plus imports; in percentages)

United Kingdom		United States		Germany		Denmark		Norway		Japan	
		1799	11.7								
1805–19	8.4										
		1809	6.1								
				1802–30	14.0						
1820–29	8.5	*1819*	9.0								
		1829	6.9								
1830–39	10.4										
		1839	8.3								
1840–49	12.6	*1849*	6.8								
		1859	7.3								
1850–59	17.1										
		1869	5.3								
1860–69	26.9										
		1879	8.0								
1870–79	29.9			*1870–79*	22.7	*1870*	23.5				
		1889	7.0							*1885–94*	8.2
1880–89	29.5			*1880–89*	16.5	*1880*	28.8				
		1899	6.3							*1895–1904*	13.6
1890–99	27.9			*1890–99*	14.9	*1890*	29.9				
		1909	5.6							*1905–14*	16.2
1900–09	26.6			*1900–09*	17.3	*1900*	35.7	*1900*	22.1		
		1919	9.2								
1910–13	29.4					*1910*	40.8	*1910*	24.0		
						1920	26.3	*1920*	28.3		
1927–29	24.7	*1929*	5.5	*1928*	18.0	*1930*	31.8	*1930*	19.8	*1920–29*	17.3
1930–38	17.1	*1939*	3.8	*1938*	7.3	*1938*	24.5	*1938*	16.9	*1930–38*	18.6
1946–49	17.1	*1949*	4.3			*1950*	32.1	*1948*	20.5		
1950–56	23.2	*1959*	4.1	*1954–59*	19.1	*1958*	32.5	*1956*	27.3	*1952, 1958*	12.1

France		*Netherlands*		*Italy*		*Canada*		*Sweden*	
1841–50	8.0								
1851–60	12.5								
1861–70	15.5			*1864–73*	10.0			*1861–68*	11.0
1871–80	15.5			*1874–83*	11.0	*1870–79*	17.0	*1869–78*	15.5
1881–90	16.5			*1884–93*	10.0	*1880–89*	14.5	*1879–88*	17.5
1891–1900	15.0			*1894–1903*	11.0	*1890–99*	12.5	*1889–98*	17.5
1901–10	16.5	*1900–08*	51.0	*1904–1913*	13.0	*1900–09*	18.0	*1899–1908*	16.5
		1909–18	43.0			*1910–19*	22.0	*1909–18*	16.0
1920–28	24.5	*1919–28*	26.0	*1919–28*	12.5	*1920–29*	16.0	*1919–28*	15.0
1929–38	12.0	*1929–38*	21.0	*1929–38*	13.5	*1930–39*	13.0	*1929–38*	13.5
1946–51	12.5	*1944–53*	29.0	*1944–53*	13.5	*1945–54*	15.5	*1939–48*	11.5
				1949–54	10.5			*1950–54*	15.0

Sources: Figures for the United Kingdom, United States, Germany, Denmark, Norway, and Japan derived from Deutsch and Eckstein, "National Industrialization and the Declining Share of the International Economic Sector, 1890–1959," pp. 267–99. Quinquennial averages have been averaged to obtain decade averages, and the trade ratio (exports plus imports in relation to income) has been divided by two, to obtain an average of exports and imports in relation to national income. Figures for France, the Netherlands, Italy, Canada, and Sweden represent ratios of average exports plus imports to national income plus imports. They are thus a different measure than the first five, and not comparable in magnitude. They have been derived from Kuznets, *Six Lectures on Economic Growth,* pp. 101–03, and have been treated in the same way as those for the other countries.

FIGURE 11–1. *Ratio of Foreign Trade to National Income, 1799–1959*

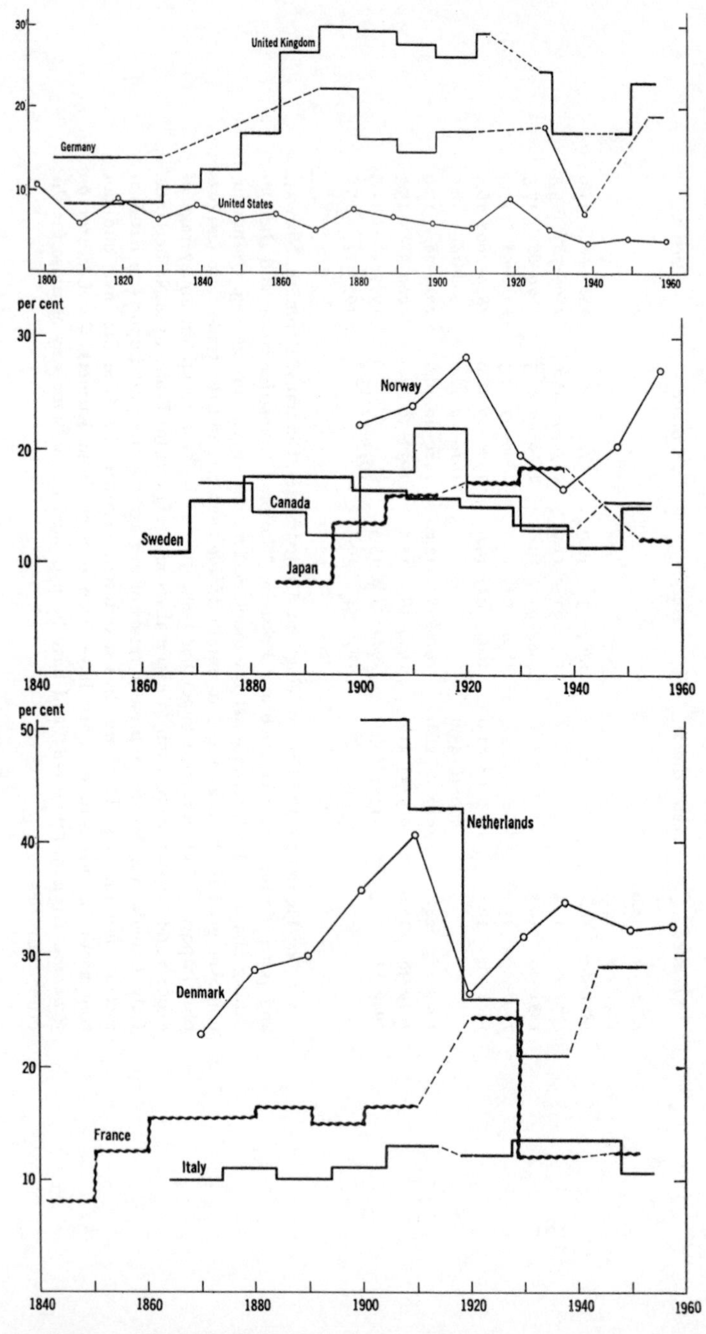

Sources: See Table 11–2.

ing to new heights, as in Britain in 1870–79 and 1910–13. A German peak was equally apparent in 1870–79, but was reapproached after World War II. Norway again made an impressive reversal after the last war, which brought the ratio well above the 1913 peak. And in Canada and Italy the ratio is fairly stable.

More detailed study, especially of the separate behavior of exports and imports through time, would be useful, if we could afford to go into the particulars, as we cannot. We may conclude that while the existence of a law of declining foreign trade has been established for developed countries only very weakly, it nevertheless exists. War, boom and depression, commercial policy, or particular patterns of trade at particular international conjunctures may interrupt, overwhelm, or distort the operation of the law; but it plays a role nonetheless. Why? How?

THE RISE OF FOREIGN TRADE

The ratio of foreign trade to national income rises when a country enters more fully into the world economy. This entry may take place as trade opens up for the first time, or it may represent an expansion of the extent of trade in response to reduced costs of transport. Specialization and exchange increase. In backward economies, monetary exchanges spread, and consumption, which had been based on subsistence, is partly supplied from abroad.

How far exports will rise depends in part on the relationships running from trade to economic growth, a subject reserved for the next chapter. Something depends upon whence the stimulus for growth emanates—from abroad or within the economy—and something more on how rapidly the economy reacts to such stimulus. But of course other elements play a role—the skewness of resources, size in space, capital movements, and so on.

But the ratio of imports to national income rises, unless restrained by commercial policy, for a number of reasons. Growth brings new needs which cannot initially be supplied locally, such as raw materials and capital equipment, new appetites through demonstration effect and rising income, and frequently new capacity to import through capital borrowings.

The new needs and appetites are likely to continue to increase imports as income grows, but beyond a certain point the rise is likely to be slower than the increase in incomes. Only occasionally are imports an inferior good, which declines absolutely as domestic income rises. (See Table 8–3.) When the income elasticity of demand for imports will change from greater than one to less than one, for a given country, depends upon a variety of circumstances.

GROWTH AND IMPORTS

In the first place, there is Engel's law. If imports consist of foodstuffs and simple materials such as textile fibers, whereas domestic production comprises more complex types of articles, Engel's law is likely to cause domestic production to grow faster than imports. It may be some time before the average country gets to the position of having satisfied its basic needs for food and clothing where the income elasticity of its imports is lower than that of domestic output; and in the earliest stages of development Engel's law may be working in the opposite sense to expand imports (of food) faster than domestic consumption. But at some relatively early stage of growth, Engel's law is likely to lend a hand in support of the law of diminishing foreign trade.

Secondly, and as an early specific manifestation of Engel's law, growth requires an increase in fixed capital which consists largely of construction. Some items of social overhead capital have a significant equipment component which could be imported, but for most of them—roads, ports, schools, and so on, construction dominates, and this must be provided locally. As expenditure increasingly shifts in favor of capital items, there is a presumption that it will turn from imported to domestic suppliers.

This is no more than a presumption, however. Domestic capital formation can be increased while maintaining or even increasing the ratio of imports to national expenditure by borrowing from abroad and shifting resources within the economy. Food formerly raised at home can be imported, while erstwhile farmers are shifted to capital formation. Nonetheless, there is likely to be a shift to domestic expenditure because of capital formation.

Third comes the growth of services in national income. Some services are supplied internationally—ocean shipping, insurance, tourism—but the bulk of them—entertainment, the liberal professions, household service, commerce, internal transport, and government—are normally furnished by domestic factors. The capital component of the railroad system may be foreign, and in colonial economies the manpower used in government. Here too, therefore, it is impossible to be categorical. But in developing countries, labor employed in services rises from something like 24 per cent of the total supply to 45 per cent, as income per capita rises from $100 to $1,700,[5] and this implies a substantial proportionate diversion of expenditure from imports to domestic markets. It would be useful to correct the data in Table 11–2 to include

5. Ibid., p. 45.

services along with exports and imports, and particularly to take account of the very high income elasticity of demand for tourist services (and of the possibility that interest and dividends on foreign investment would modify the export ratio). But a number of imported services, such as transport, are subject to the law of declining foreign trade, either because they are linked to commodity trade or because of the substitution of domestic for foreign sources of supply. It is unlikely that the overall result would be greatly modified.

Fourth is the normal process of import substitution. There is much talk in underdeveloped countries today of policies of import substitution, particularly in consumers' goods. It must not be forgotten, however, that the process is an entirely natural one in the course of economic growth, and takes place without, though in some cases it may be speeded up by, barriers to importing. Part of the process is simply a question of location economies. Many economic processes are market-oriented. When a market grows to a certain size, as indicated by total income, with a certain minimum income per capita, opportunity has been created for the local development of these processes. Thus Denmark and New Zealand, which are regarded as agricultural states because of their concentration on agricultural exports, have roughly 35 per cent of their labor forces engaged in mining, manufacturing, and construction, compared with close to 20 per cent in agriculture, forestry, and fishing,[6] because of the spillover of income from agricultural production into nonfood consumption and the pull of the market. Douglass North has described the process in detail in his article on the growth of

6. Simon Kuznets, "Quantitative Aspects of the Economic Growth of Nations, II, Industrial Distribution of National Product and Labor Force," *Economic Development and Cultural Change, 5,* Supplement (1957), 75, 80.

the Pacific Northwest, dealing with the development of local industry subsequent to the expansion of the export industries of timber and mining.[7] And, in his *The Strategy of Economic Development,* based partly on his experience in Colombia, Hirschman has indicated how the growth of imports precedes the establishment of a domestic industry by demonstrating the existence of a market.[8] Nurkse had suggested that it was difficult to start domestic industries in developing countries because of lack of demand.[9] Hirschman countered that the growth of imports proves the existence of a market. Refineries are built when imports of refined products get to a certain volume, and breweries when beer imports become substantial.

An econometric study by Hollis Chenery has gone beyond Hirschman and North, and beyond the study of particular cases, to generalize more widely.[10] Examining the experience of forty countries, Chenery concludes that growth in production typically outstrips growth in domestic demand, and that the two variables are brought back into equilibrium by import substitution. This process, he concludes, lies at the heart of economic growth. Once growth has gone a certain distance, countries tend to become less rather than more specialized. Lord Keynes in fact once expressed the view that economic development was likely to eliminate substantial differences between the productive capacities of various

7. Douglass C. North, "Location Theory and Regional Economic Growth," *Journal of Political Economy, 63* (1955), 243–58.

8. Albert O. Hirschman, *The Strategy of Economic Development* (New Haven, Yale University Press, 1958), esp. pp. 120–22.

9. *Some Problems of Capital Formation in Underdeveloped Countries.*

10. "Patterns of Industrial Growth," *American Economic Review, 50* (1960), 624–54.

countries, and hence the basis for trade.[11] This seems to be far from the case, however. For, while growth continues, needs and appetites rise too. Industrial countries trade with each other on the basis of specialization in industrial products. Some offset to increasing proportions of services in national product, increased consumption of market-oriented production, and increased capacity to provide a wide variety of products at home is provided by the tendency of developing countries to want highly differentiated products in consumption and investment. Differentiation provides further room for specialization and exchange, especially with long-run decreasing-cost curves.[12]

TECHNOLOGY

Chapter 6 has already discussed how technological change can create and kill trade, and mentioned that Professor Hicks believes that its effect was stronger in the former direction in the nineteenth century, in the latter in the twentieth. There is a risk that this discussion may have left an implication that innovation is generally either import-substituting or export-creating for the country in which it occurs. This is, of course, not the case. Innovation can create new demands for imports, as the pneumatic tire and the atomic bomb amply demonstrate. An innovation which destroyed exports would be more difficult to find, but perhaps the jet

11. John Maynard Keynes, "National Self-Sufficiency," *Yale Review*, *22* (1933), 755–69. W. Arthur Lewis argues that ultimately trade will be confined to products in which countries have comparative advantages based on natural resources. See "Economic Development with Unlimited Supplies of Labour," *Manchester School*, *22* (1954), 139–91. See also D. M. Bensusan-Butt, "A Model of Trade and Accumulation," *American Economic Review*, *44* (1954), 511–29.

12. See above, p. 70.

aircraft, which increased United States demand for kerosene, a one-time export, will serve to illustrate the possibilities. What are the net effects likely to be?

It is generally agreed that imitation in underdeveloped countries tends to reduce trade, as domestic production is substituted for imports, along the lines of the North-Hirschman-Chenery mechanism just discussed; and that innovation on balance tends to favor exports and to depress imports. If innovation spreads very rapidly from one country to another and there is no clear factor preponderance in inputs to give a sharp comparative advantage, innovation may substitute for imports of natural products everywhere at once, and thus lead to a reduction of trade.

But atabrine, Buna-S, synthetic nitrates, nylon, dynel, detergents, and chicle do not represent the only possible effect of innovation on trade in natural-resource products. Such innovations will produce an absolute reduction in trade. But a relative reduction has also been achieved through the increased complexity of manufactured goods in normal use, which means that more and more value is added to a given output of natural products, whether of domestic or foreign origin. One dollar's worth of iron ore was incorporated in six dollars' worth of goods in 1900 and twelve dollars' worth in 1950.[13] For the industrial countries that import primary products and produce industrial goods at home, this means a continuous reduction in the imports–national-product ratio. The industrial goods may be in brisk demand abroad in other industrial countries, with the result that after time, the exports–income—and eventually the imports–income—ratio rises again. But underdeveloped countries could argue that whether or not there is a tendency for trade to grow

13. President's Materials Policy Committee (Paley Commission), *Resources for Freedom, 1* (Washington, D.C., G.P.O., 1952), 7.

among industrialized developed countries, imports of this group from primary producers decline relatively. This neglects depletion in developed countries, and the possibility of growing imports of relatively elementary manufactures which become increasingly complex. Leaving these aside, however, there is a possibility that the law of declining foreign trade may hold for no single industrial country (though by and large the figures seem to indicate that it does for most), while holding for industrial countries as a group versus the primary producers.

PROTECTION

Finally, it is suggested in some quarters that developed countries are slow to transform out of those commodities in which they have a new comparative disadvantage. Deutsch and Eckstein believe that with increasing instability as a country grows richer there is an increased tendency to interfere with the outcome of market decisions, especially when they spell unemployment or reduced income for some group.[14] Nurkse argues, on the one hand, that developed countries have a bias to agricultural protection; on the other, that the attempts of underdeveloped countries to enter new manufactured lines affect the weakest groups in developed countries, which demand national protection. These are typically, as in the textile industry, the regions and the producers who have been engaged for the longest time in a single industry, and have lost the capacity to adapt.[15] It is difficult to build a typical pattern here; the British were prepared to see the landless agricultural worker driven off the farm, and

14. "National Industrialization," pp. 297–98.

15. Ragnar Nurkse, *Patterns of Trade and Development* (Stockholm, 1959), pp. 23, 29.

the United States protects the wealthy Texas oilman. There may be something to it. Transformation in the developed countries of a sort advantageous to the underdeveloped may affect the groups which have been longest engaged in a single occupation, and therefore are effective claimants on public sympathy, or which are engaged in labor-intensive activity and would therefore pose an employment problem if the industry were allowed to collapse under the weight of imports. But it is more likely that political power is the significant variable, and it is impossible to generalize about this.[16]

GROWTH MODELS

No single comprehensive model of the process of economic growth has yet been developed, and we may usefully conclude this chapter by pointing out the implications of the principal partial models of growth for international trade. In this we recur to the discussion of Chapter 7 on the models of Burenstam Linder, Johnson, and Bhagwati.

In a society with no capacity to transform—that is, with no responsiveness to the price system—domestic growth may take place anyway. This may be both growth of population and growth of capital. Output will get larger, but in the same lines as before. Imports may kill off the import-competing

16. Note, for example, the preponderant importance in American politics of Texas oil interests, which benefit from the fact that the Democratic leadership in the House, and earlier in the Senate, has been Texan in origin, and from the continuous possibility that the state may "go Republican" in a national election. In Britain, the power of the Lancashire textile industry, which led the Conservative government to seek export quotas in India, Pakistan, Hong Kong, and Japan, lay in the fact that the Conservative government in 1948 had forty-five MPs from the area whose seats had average pluralities of less than 5 per cent. The political power of farmers, as noted earlier, stems from the fact that such power is transferred more slowly than economic.

sector and make production possibilities even more skewed and specialized. Growth may ultimately make the country worse off than it has been, if the loss in the terms of trade from increased exports outweighs the increase in output. Much depends upon how skewed the original resources were, and the elasticity of foreign demand. But it is possible to end up worse off through growth. This is an extreme case, and I must confess I have no examples that fit it without substantial qualification.

Observe that it makes an important difference for trade whether growth proceeds along the lines of the Harrod-Domar model, under which income rises as a result of exponentially expanding capital formation, or of an Abramowitz-Solow model (so-called after two economists whose statistical investigations have emphasized the contribution to growth of technological change). In the Harrod-Domar model, as Johnson was the first to point out,[17] growth in one country enlarges trade through raising income, as well as probably shifting comparative advantage by changing factor proportions through capital accumulation. Such a shift need not take place: capital may be divided among industries in exactly the same proportions as before. If a shift takes place, moreover, it need not favor the capital-intensive industry if there are complementarities as well as substitutions among factors, and capital is invested in the land-intensive or the labor-intensive sectors. On the demand side, it is necessary to take into account income elasticities, as well as rates of income growth: if two areas are growing along Harrod-Domar lines, the faster-growing will pull the slower one

17. Harry G. Johnson, "Equilibrium Growth in an International Economy," *Canadian Journal of Economics and Political Science, 19* (1953), 478–500, republished as chap. 5 of his *International Trade and Economic Growth* (London, 1958).

along through trade unless the difference in rates of growth is offset by opposite differences in income elasticities of demand for imports. Thus the European Economic Community exerts pressure for growth on Britain, for whose products its demand is income-elastic, but may not do so for primary producers.

The effects of technological change on trade under an Abramowitz-Solow model will vary depending upon whether a given country is a leading innovator, a former leader falling behind, a "catching-up" country, or a continuous laggard, and whether the innovation or imitation takes place at home or abroad.[18] Most of these cases have been covered above and in Chapter 6, but a further word may be due to the example of the United States which was a technological leader from World War I to about ten years after World War II, and has recently seen the closing of the technological gap between it and Western Europe. Innovation at home in the leader has two effects on trade: it gives a fillip to exports, but it hurts imports—by more effective competition and by lifting the level of demand to the kinds of goods not readily produced abroad. Apart from the evident effect on the balance of trade, it becomes difficult to say what the net effect will be on the ratio of trade turnover to income. In the United States the trade-destroying effects seem to have dominated, especially as foreign countries were prevented by balance-of-payments difficulties from obtaining all the United States goods they wanted. As imitation and innovation abroad reduced the United States' lead after World War II, however, exports fell off in the face of strong competition, and imports grew, particularly of manufactured goods. Here the net effect was a rise in the ratio of foreign trade to income.

18. Burenstam Linder, *An Essay on Trade and Transformation*, pp. 142 ff., offers some suggestive if brief remarks on this subject.

There are, unfortunately, no simple answers to the effects of growth on trade. The full answer in any case can be given only after all the variables have been specified. This difference, however, does seem fundamental: in Harrod-Domar growth there may be expansion of capacity in exports, and probably to a less extent in import-competing lines; but the major effect is the rise of income which spills over into imports. The two-country, two-commodity model, in which growth has to occur in exports or in import-competing industry, is misleading, since it overlooks the possibility that growth will affect trade not through enlarging capacity but only by expanding income. Under the Abramowitz-Solow model there will be increases in income which enlarge the demand for imports, and technological advances, such as in missiles, which are unrelated to trade. The major effect, however, is likely to be new exports, more competition in existing exports, and new or more effective import-competing capacity. Harrod-Domar growth generally worsens the balance of payments; Abramowitz-Solow growth generally improves it. This seems to be the fundamental explanation—leaving aside all necessary qualification—for the recent disparate balance-of-payments behavior of Britain and the United States, on the one hand, and Germany, France, Italy, and Japan, on the other.

12 THE IMPACT OF TRADE ON GROWTH

THREE MODELS

We turn now from the impact of growth on trade to the converse: how does foreign trade affect economic growth? Here it may be useful to distinguish three broad models into which real cases may with difficulty be classified: where trade is a leading, a balancing, or a lagging sector of the economy. In the first, the stimulus to economic development comes from abroad. Exports rise and contribute an incentive to the establishment and expansion of other activities. In the lagging model, the stimulus to development is internal, and trade may slow down growth. In the intermediate case, adjustment of trade keeps pace with domestic transformation. It will be of particular importance to consider Ragnar Nurkse's view that external stimuli to growth and industrialization were inherent in the pattern of the nineteenth century, but are no longer relevant to the twentieth, except perhaps in oil. To judge this question, it will be useful to examine not only the demand characteristics of export commodities, which interested Nurkse, but also the supply.

EXPORT-LED GROWTH

There is no difficulty in illustrating the model of export-led growth. Great Britain furnishes the prime example, both in the way that exports of first textiles and then iron and coal stimulated the growth of income in Britain, and in the reflex action of British imports in spreading growth throughout the nineteenth century. Some growth was diffused abroad through technical assistance and lending. Britain contributed in this way to the development of France and Western Europe, before moving overseas, and France in turn assisted Germany, Austria, Switzerland, Italy, Spain, and the rest of Europe.[1] But other growth was communicated as well, or perhaps initially and primarily, through the impact of British demands for primary production. The United States was an early recipient of this stimulus in cotton; later the Areas of Recent Settlement, as Hilgerdt called them, were turned to for wheat, wool, meat (after refrigerator ships had been developed about 1875), timber, and minerals; Sweden felt the demand for timber, wood pulp, and iron ore; the Netherlands for meat and cheese; Denmark, butter, eggs, and bacon. The tropics were largely left aside from the mainstream of this early demand, although isolated impacts were felt in tea, spices, tin, and later rubber.

How does export-demand work? First, exports grow. This

1. Rondo E. Cameron, *France and the Economic Development of Europe, 1800–1914* (Princeton, Princeton University Press, 1961).

gives rise to new demands in the exporting country, both for inputs to contribute to the physical expansion of production, and as a result of the increase in incomes of factors of production. Where economies of scale result in a reduced price for the output, new production may be stimulated, at home or abroad, using the good as an input. Pressure on domestic capacity may stimulate technological change: the development in steel of the Bessemer process in 1856 and of the Siemens-Martin process ten years later were results of export pressure.[2] Such pressure may also call the attention of entrepreneurs to investment opportunities, and stimulate growth by raising the level of investment.[3] Expansion of exports can thus lead to growth through stimulating technical change and investment, or by spilling demand over into other sectors. Rostow has suggested that the growth process involves a leading sector which communicates its growth to the rest of the economy.[4] In the export-led model, exports are a leading sector.

But not every development of exports leads to economic growth, as the mention of cotton indicates. The rapid expansion of a primary product export can lead to economic development, as Douglass North has suggested.[5] But it need not, as the American South proves.[6]

Current economic literature makes much of demand, and especially the forces of Engel's law, increasing economy of

2. H. J. Habakkuk, "Free Trade and Commercial Expansion, 1858–1870," in *The Cambridge History of the British Empire, 2* (Cambridge, Eng., Cambridge University Press, 1940), 802.

3. See above, pp. 186–87.

4. W. W. Rostow, "The Take-Off into Self-Sustained Growth," *Economic Journal, 66* (1956), 25–48.

5. "Location Theory."

6. Douglass C. North, "Agriculture in Regional Economic Growth," *Journal of Farm Economics, 12* (1959), 943–51.

raw material inputs, low price elasticities, and so on, as discussed in Chapter 11. What has been neglected is the work of a Canadian economic historian, Harold Innis, who propounded a "staple theory" of Canadian economy growth.[7] Cod, furs, timber, wheat, and minerals had different effects on economic growth in Canada owing to their different physical characteristics. Accident could play a significant role: British settlement occurred in Newfoundland and Nova Scotia in advance of French (or Portuguese) settlement because France and Portugal possessed abundant and cheap salt which enabled them to salt their cod caught off the banks "green," i.e. on shipboard; whereas the British, without salt, were forced to go ashore to dry the fish in the sun. Furs were a poor commodity for growth because they required large inputs of land, on the one hand, and used little cargo space, on the other. With timber and wheat exports, vacant cargo capacity was available on the westbound voyage, which encouraged immigration. At the same time, however, it has been pointed out that cheap backhaul rates for commodities discourage local production of market-oriented goods, since the protection afforded by distance is reduced.[8]

Timber, minerals, and especially wheat had positive effects on Canadian economic growth. Wheat stimulated immigration and railroad construction, both of which had external effects on growth. In addition, it gave rise to the establishment of a farm-machinery industry. Timber and min-

7. See, among other works, *Problems of Staple Production in Canada* (Toronto, 1933). For a useful summary of Innis' work see R. E. Caves and R. H. Holton, *The Canadian Economy* (Cambridge, Mass., 1959), chaps. 3, 4.

8. Douglass C. North, "Ocean Freight Rates and Economic Development, 1750–1913," *Journal of Economic History, 18* (1958), 546–47.

ing spurred the growth of intensive agriculture to feed the settlements; and mining gradually led to industries for smelting, refining, and fabricating.

To what extent do these external dynamic effects follow from the production for export of all commodities? A particularly striking contrast is between, on the one hand, milk, butter and, to a lesser degree, cheese, which can form a leading sector in growth and communicate progress to the rest of the economy, and, on the other, meat production, which does not appear to do so.[9] The former are labor-intensive, and require a sturdy, independent group of peasants or farmers; the latter is land-intensive, and flourishes with a feudal type of society that does not encourage consumption. The contrast runs between Denmark, New Zealand, Switzerland, and the Netherlands, on the one hand, and Argentina on the other, or between Wisconsin and Texas. The density of settlement is an important consideration for cattle, wool, and, in Africa, even ordinary crops. In the African Pre-Cambrian shield, according to Egbert deVries,[10] the support of a family requires not just three acres, as in Asia, but fifty, or even a hundred. The result is that it is impossible to achieve settlements dense enough to establish villages, which are a prerequisite for efficiency in distribution and administration, and hence in development.

Sociologists have drawn distinctions among tropical field crops. Coffee is of high value relative to its weight and can therefore be produced in remote areas, accessible only by mule or jeep. It does not give rise to roads, with their external economies. Where it is organized in plantations, it needs

9. A distinction should be made between raising cattle on the range and fattening stock in feeder lots. The latter is much more labor-intensive and requires less land.

10. Communicated in conversation.

large amounts of labor during the harvest season; and, like sugar, it has a long "dead season."[11] As a bulk product, sugar needs transport, but the frequent availability of excellent harbors in the islands of the West Indies minimizes the need to construct roads or railroads, which produce more frequent face-to-face contacts. DeVries notes the different technological demands made by different crops on their producers. Annual crops present a continuous challenge to improve productivity through seed selection, crop rotation, application of fertilizer, irrigation of dry land and drainage of wet, and development of machinery. The scarcer and more expensive the labor, the greater the challenge to apply machinery. Thus development proceeded more rapidly where there were immigrant farmers than in densely populated tropical countries where there were none, or in labor-intensive crops, like cotton, sugar, and coffee, which could be produced in the early stages only in labor-intensive ways calling for slaves or native workers. But in tree crops the technical demands on the producer are limited under any circumstances, and technical change can occur only by means of an intense investment effort, likely to require the leadership of government. With coffee, cocoa, rubber, or wine grapes, the trees, bushes, and vines take a number of years to reach maturity before they bear, and then remain in production over an extended period. During this period there is little that can be done to improve product or affect productivity. Defensive efforts may be called for to combat disease. To produce a new and more productive strain, as in rubber replanting in Malaya, requires organized research and a capi-

11. P. N. Rosenstein-Rodan has pointed out to me that in Costa Rica and Honduras annual crops are planted in the shade of coffee trees, set out in widely spaced rows, which evens out the demand for labor. In more specialized Guatemala this offset is lacking.

tal investment effort, both of which are likely to be beyond the capabilities of the individual planter.

Thus primary products have different effects on economic growth as a result of their inputs and the resultant income distribution, their sociological aspects, and technical requirements. It is increasingly recognized that the same holds true for industrial goods. Commenting on the complaint of the French that their country fell behind because of lack of coal, Professor Parker has suggested that coal was needed less as fuel, or as an input of steel, than because of its effect in encouraging the development of a dense railroad and canal network for its distribution, with important side effects for development.[12] Richard Eckaus, who is exploring the educational requirements of economic growth, mentions as a tentative first finding that in Italy, textile workers are like farmers[13] in that they are good for nothing else. They lack capacity to encourage transformation. In France, the Lorraine area is finding that the production of iron ore, pig iron, and even steel does not lead to spreading development, at least in this instance,[14] and Lyons complains that the chemical industry, set down in the countryside, with research offices in urban areas and its head offices in Paris, fails to serve as a "growing point," or a *pôle de croissance*.[15] Finally it is

12. Parker, "Comment" on Kindleberger, "International Trade and Investment, and Resource Use," in Spengler, *Natural Resources and Economic Growth*.

13. A distinction should be made between farmers in a labor-intensive society, such as Italy, and those in Areas of Recent Settlement, who have developed a capacity to handle machinery. Thus in World War II, it was found that farmers made the worst soldiers in the German army and the best in the Canadian.

14. R. Nistri and C. Prêcheur, *La Région du nord et du nord-est* (Paris, Presses Universitaires de France, 1959), pp. 116, 127 ff..

15. J. Labasse and M. Laferrère, *La Région lyonnaise* (Paris, Presses Universitaires de France, 1960), p. 137.

striking that Belgian observers believe that the economic growth of their country is impeded by concentration in large-scale industry with standard processes and labor-saving machinery, but involving little technical change or high-grade specialized labor: steel plate and wire, soda ash, nitrate fertilizer, metal refining, glass, and cement, along with textiles, in contrast with the more stimulating industries of electrical and general engineering, synthetic chemicals, pharmaceuticals, etc.[16] Table 12–1 lists some leading Belgian exports and suggests the problem.

Economists have not studied these linkages sufficiently to be able to predict how they work in detail. Commodities differ significantly in their requirements for labor, transport, and machinery, and in their effects on income distribution (and consumer demand and savings), technological change, and social capacity to produce entrepreneurs. The effects of some of these on growth will be opposed: with limited good land and cheap labor (as in cotton), rent and profits will be high and savings substantial; but the social system of the plantation may not be conducive to investment in other enterprises. Contrariwise, a crop produced with scarce labor, like wheat, may stimulate consumption but hold back capital formation.

These effects are not immutable. Leaving aside for the time being the possibility of taxing its profits, oil production and refining might well have limited potential for spreading growth were it not for the efforts of oil companies and the

16. A. Lamfalussy, *Investment and Growth in Mature Economies* (London, Macmillan, 1961); Roger Dehem, "La Propension à la croissance de l'économie belge," lecture given before the Royal Society of Political Economy of Belgium, Nov. 22, 1960; and the *Report* for the year 1958–59 of the Compagnie d'Outremer pour l'Industrie et la Finance, Brussels, Nov. 26, 1959.

TABLE 12–1. *Leading Exports of Belgium–Luxembourg, 1959*

Commodity	*Percentage of Total Exports by Value*
Iron and steel	22.8
Textiles (yarn, cloth, clothing)	13.7
Jewelry	5.5
Electrical machinery	5.4
Other machinery	4.6
Metal manufactures	4.3
Artificial fertilizer	4.0
Petroleum products	3.6
Unwrought copper	3.2
Glass (not including glassware)	2.6
Total	69.7

Source: O.E.E.C. *Statistical Bulletin,* Series D, Belgium-Luxembourg (January–December 1959).

obligations imposed on them by host governments to train local employees. This is because oil production, like the chemicals already mentioned, is highly capital-intensive, using a foreign, standardized technology and specialized skills of labor; what little local labor it uses will have difficulty in absorbing these skills and technology. The Gezira cotton scheme in the Anglo-Egyptian Sudan, which was a substantial success, might have gone further in its preparation of that area for economic development if it had envisaged the development of light industry along with the peasant production of cotton.[17] And of course differential tariffs on exports of raw materials but not on finished products, or on imports of finished products but not on raw materials, can create or stimulate linkages to spread the growth effects.

This conclusion is not wholly satisfactory. Exports can

17. Arthur Gaitskell, *Gezira, a Story of Development in the Sudan* (London, Faber and Faber, 1959).

lead to growth, but they need not. If they are to do so, there must be capital formation, technical change, reallocation of resources. The larger the gains from trade, given these processes, the faster and more certainly will growth proceed. And for a given gain from trade, the more capital formation, technical change, and transformation, the better. But large potential gains from trade without capacity to make use of them, or large capacities without gains from trade to serve as a basis for changes, will not help.

In discussing the spread of railroads in France in the middle of the nineteenth century, A. L. Dunham has suggested that the various parts of the country were so much alike—wheat was grown, for example, in eighty-eight of the ninety departments, and occupied more than half the tillable soil in all but ten of these—that the gains from increased internal trade were limited, which held back economic development.[18] Other writers emphasize the French family firm and its effect on capacity to transform. But, other things equal, the more skewed the resources up to a certain point, the larger the gains from trade and the greater the contribution to growth. The mechanism by which these gains from trade are transmuted into capital formation or technical change and transmitted from the export sector to other sectors will vary from case to case. One relevant means is government action, which may tax the export sector and invest in other activities. This is particularly relevant to oil, where, as noticed, the capital forming and transforming mechanism, left to itself, might fail to operate efficaciously.

18. *The Industrial Revolution in France, 1815–1848* (New York, Exposition Press, 1955). See also his review of Charles Morazé, *La France bourgeoise: xviii–xx siècles*, in *Journal of Economic History, 6* (1946), 197–99.

Nurkse believed that export-led growth is a thing of the past.[19] Apart from oil, which as discoveries pile up and the price drops may prove less and less an exception, underdeveloped countries today are unlikely to duplicate the process followed in the nineteenth century. The change in demand factors has been mentioned. In supply, the major differences would seem to run between the nineteenth-century Areas of Recent Settlement, where labor was scarce despite immigration but land abundant, and where rents were low and wages high; and the twentieth-century overcrowded countries of Asia and Africa, where wages are low and rents high. Latin America falls into neither of these categories. Argentina was held back by the social system inherent in ranching, Brazil perhaps by the plantation system, which favors high profits and rents, or perhaps by the limited technical demands of the crop. But in these matters much research remains to be completed before we understand the connections in all their complexity.

TRADE AS A BALANCING SECTOR

It goes without saying that trade is always a balancing factor in the sense of filling the gap between production and consumption, if we ignore changes in stocks. More is intended here. The process of growth poses a number of questions of balance. Foreign trade can assist in their solution. In particular it has been suggested by Nurkse that developing countries cannot industrialize one product at a time because of lack of demand: the increased income from the single product is spent on a wide number of goods, and it is therefore impossible for an underdeveloped country to start

19. Nurkse, *Patterns of Trade and Development,* pp. 19, 20.

off on production of a single industrial product on an efficient scale, because it cannot absorb the output.[20] Production for the foreign market is one way to escape this dilemma, along with production for the domestic market of commodities revealed by the import statistics to be demanded in sufficient quantities.

The usual case cited is Japan. Exports did not lead economic growth in Japan, but provided close support. On the one hand, there was the fortunate expansion of the world demand for silk, resulting from the expansion of world income and the spread of the silkworm disease, pébrine, in Europe. On the other hand, effective organization of the cotton textile industry enabled Japanese manufacturers to expand the sale of simple textiles in competition with Britain, to extend manufacturing in Japan, and so to acquire the foreign exchange necessary for imported raw materials, fuel, and capital equipment. With the passage of time, and especially after World War II, Japanese exports developed in complexity and value added per unit of primary product, as shown in Table 4–3, to put Japan in the ranks of developed countries as far as the structure of its trade, if not the level of income per capita, is concerned.

Another model of balancing trade has been applied to Great Britain. From 1850 to 1875 the British economy can be said to have conformed to the export-led model. After 1875, however, according to W. Arthur Lewis,[21] the rate of expansion of exports decreased from 6 per cent a year to 2 per cent. This could be, and has been, taken to have slowed

20. Nurkse, *Some Problems of Capital Formation in Underdeveloped Countries,* chap. 1.

21. *Theory of Economic Growth;* and idem., "International Competition in Manufactures," *American Economic Review, Papers and Proceedings, 47* (1957), 578–87.

down British economic growth directly,[22] as if exports, once having led, must continue to lead through all time, leaving domestic investment, government expenditure, and consumption always as dependent variables. But Lewis' reasoning is more complex. In his view an attempt was made to shift investment to domestic industry. This raised national income and increased imports of foodstuffs (because land was in short supply) and of raw materials. To prevent the balance of payments from turning adverse, it would have been necessary for exports to have expanded in line with rising imports, as called for by a model of balanced foreign trade. Manufacturers, however, lacked the "irresistible urge to invest" in new industry, plus an interest in, and techniques appropriate to, expanding exports. Exports failed to keep pace, the balance of payments weakened, and it became necessary to slow down industrialization to the rate at which exports provided the appropriate balance. The result was that savings could not be used at home and were invested abroad.

This account conforms to a reasonable presentation of the "lagging sector" model, where exports fail to balance, until the mention of capital exports at the very end. How it is possible to have too small exports to finance desired domestic investment, and at the same time foreign lending and a balance of payments surplus on current account, is difficult to see. The fault would seem to have lain less with too little exports, than with too much exports of the wrong things, a refusal to alter product or production methods as European and North American markets were shut down, and a preference for diverting standardized unchanged exports of textiles,

22. See, for example, J. R. Meyer, "An Input-Output Approach to Evaluating the Influence of Exports on British Industrial Production in the Late 19th Century," *Explorations in Entrepreneurial History, 8* (1955), 12–34.

rails, galvanized sheet, tin plate, and ships to new, often protected markets. One could in fact make a case that too great an expansion of (the wrong) exports slowed down growth.[23] The parallel with the Belgian problem cited earlier is striking. In both instances, moreover, there is a resemblance to the fossilization seen by Myint in plantations. Where the training effect of exports is below that of domestic industries, short-run comparative advantage may not furnish the best path to growth.

TRADE AS A LAGGING SECTOR

Our inability to find a handicap to domestic expansion in lagging exports when the current account shows a substantial surplus does not mean that failure of exports to expand may not slow down economic expansion. In the view of Prebisch,[24] Myrdal,[25] Singer,[26] and possibly to some extent of Nurkse,[27] growth in the underdeveloped countries must proceed through domestic industrialization, since there is little chance of reliance on export-led growth. Domestic investment will increase demand for capital equipment from abroad, and for basic materials, including fuel. Since exports grow but slowly, and capital borrowing is impossible or ex-

23. See my "Foreign Trade and Economic Growth: Lessons from Britain and France, 1850 to 1913," *Economic History Review, 14* (1961), 289–305.

24. United Nations Economic and Social Council, Economic Commission for Latin America (Raul Prebisch), *The Economic Development of Latin America and Its Principal Problems* (Lake Success, 1950).

25. G. Myrdal, *The International Economy: Problems and Prospects* (New York, 1956), esp. chap. 13.

26. "Distribution of Gains between Investing and Borrowing Countries."

27. *Patterns of Trade.*

pensive, it is necessary to cut down on imports of consumers' goods. Total imports will not decline under this policy of "import substitution." But their composition will change away from consumption items in favor of machinery and primary products.

Nurkse assents to this reasoning, but adds that the policy calls for a simultaneous improvement in agricultural production, and possibly over a wide range of consumers' goods, to prevent imbalance on the home front. If agricultural productivity is not increased, for example, the increased income from domestic investment in leading sectors and import substitutes will be spent partly for foodstuffs, and it will raise prices and exert further pressure for imports or cause inflation in this sector.

The form of the argument sees the causation running from growth to trade as in the previous chapter. Trade can be a serious constraint on growth unless steps are taken to forestall it. Capital imports and foreign aid are two means of doing so, though they fall outside our subject. Import substitution in consumers' goods may be another.

But there is a danger in accepting the import-substitution therapy too readily. Economists are still a long way from knowing all that needs to be known about the connections running between trade and economic growth. It is a vast oversimplification to think that we are limited to these three models, and that if exports fail to lead or to balance domestic investment, it is automatically necessary to cut imports (in the absence of aid or loans). This implies a Harrod-Domar model of growth, in which demand always leads. And as we observed in the previous chapter, there are other models of growth, such as the Abramowitz-Solow, in which supply leads. If import-competing industry stands on the brink of economies of scale, a tariff which restricts imports may lead to expanding domestic growth. This is the optimal outcome of import substitution. But if domestic entrepreneurs are sluggish and timid about applying new techniques or devising them, it may just be that increased imports will help by shaking them up. The competitive effect of imports can be important, and, where it is, import substitution is exactly the wrong medicine.

One case in point is the Anglo-French Treaty of Commerce in 1860 and its effects in completing the conversion in France from charcoal to coal in iron and steel, from handicraft to machinery in textiles, from the cottage to the factory. The reduction of tariffs is said to have brought about the full development of the Industrial Revolution in France.[28] Another more timely example is the mutual reduction of tariffs in the European Economic Community: only part of the growth stimulated by this means will occur in expanding export industries and spillover; another significant effect will be the threat of import competition which can stimulate investment and technical change when the receptivity is there.

The major difference between the export-led growth of the nineteenth century and the lagging-export model applicable so widely in the twentieth is that demand leads in the latter, supply in the former. The difference corresponds to the difference between the Harrod-Domar and the Abramowitz-Solow models. It is also reminiscent of Wallich's distinction between Schumpeterian growth, in which the entrepreneur and production lead; and Duesenberry growth, in which consumption and the demonstration effect are paramount.[29]

28. Dunham, *Anglo-French Treaty of Commerce,* p. 179. The spread of the railroad, of course, also helped.

29. H. Wallich, *Mainsprings of German Revival* (New Haven, Yale University Press, 1955), chap. 2.

The impact of foreign trade on growth is then indeterminate over a wide range. Trade can stimulate growth, when the demand is right abroad and the supply is right at home. It can inhibit it when the demand is wrong abroad and the supply is wrong at home. In the two intermediate cases, we do not know.

13 THE EFFECTS OF TRADE ON STABILITY

THE LOCUS OF DISTURBANCE

Whether foreign trade contributes to stability or instability in a country depends upon where the disturbance originates. If it is local—if, that is, there is a domestic crop failure or a boom or depression of domestic origin—foreign trade is likely to lend stability. If, on the other hand, the disturbance originates abroad, strong foreign trade links with the rest of the world can impart that instability to the domestic economy. Since business cycles tend to start in industrial economies, with their larger proportions of postponable expenditures in the form of capital equipment and durable consumers' goods, there is something to the generalization that foreign trade is stabilizing for industrial countries and destabilizing for countries exporting primary products.

The simplest illustration of the stabilizing action of foreign trade is to assume an internal boom. Without foreign trade, supplies of goods would be shorter, money incomes and prices would go higher. One could argue that with reduced supplies of goods, the upward spiral of spending would have to halt more quickly, so that while foreign trade reduces the amplitude of the cycle, it prolongs its duration. This is possible. But the foreign trade mechanism also applies brakes to the internal boom, through the adverse balance of payments, the loss of gold or foreign exchange, and the effects of these on the money supply, interest rates, and so on—subjects that lie outside the field of our interest. These may in fact speed up the reversal of the initial disturbance, as contrasted with the closed economy.

When a disturbance occurs abroad, foreign trade may communicate it to a country. The 1929 boom in the United States was felt throughout the world, and so was the ensuing depression.

STABILITY IN INDUSTRIAL COUNTRIES

The stabilizing or destabilizing effects of foreign trade can be analyzed at a variety of levels—in the markets for particular commodities, in broad classes of expenditure, and in income as a whole. Let us take them in order.

Assume a crop failure in a single country. Without foreign trade, the country goes hungry. The farmers may find that they do well enough—food is at least in their reach, for one thing; and they may find that the elasticity of demand for food is unity or less for the food they market, so that their incomes are stabilized without foreign trade. But the rest of the country is forced to reduce its real consumption of bread and may cut down as well on other consumption if the demand for food is inelastic. The country as a whole will find the crop failure highly upsetting. With imports available, the crop failure raises prices and attracts supplies from abroad. This will destabilize the incomes of farmers, whose fall in marketings is not now offset by a rise in prices, and almost certainly the balance of payments as well. But the net effects are stabilizing: consumption, prices, and expenditures in other sectors are maintained at steadier rates.

When a number of industrial countries have business cycles which are not very closely articulated, the spillover of demand from one to another, as the limits of domestic capacity are reached in boom, will give rise to trade which may move now in one direction, now in another. This type of trade, illustrated by changes in the gross movements of steel across the Atlantic since 1950, when the booms and depressions in the United States and Western Europe have been broadly offsetting, is at odds with the underlying concepts of comparative advantage. It nonetheless illustrates the stabilizing role of trade. The data are set forth in Table 13–1. Note that the stabilizing role could be played in foreign trade in steel across the ocean only because of the relative decline in transport costs after World War II.

At the level of classes of expenditure, the stabilizing effects of foreign trade can be illustrated with inventories, and especially inventories of primary products. If manufacturers and wholesalers observe prices of primary products going up, and in consequence start to lay in stocks—an example of elastic expectations and destabilizing speculation—the availability of supplies abroad and the spillover of inventory investment into imports helps to stabilize prices and expenditure at the same time that it destabilizes the balance of payments and communicates the instability abroad. The more markets are joined, the less erratic and excited price movements in any one market will be—provided, however, that the view of prices in each market is taken independently. If all dealers in all markets are equally affected by elastic expectations and have equal access to credit, the joining of markets has no stabilizing effect.

TABLE 13–1. *United States Transatlantic Trade in Steel, 1950–1959 (exports of semifinished and finished steel products to Western Europe; imports from Belgium-Luxembourg, Western Germany, and France; in thousands of metric tons)*

	United States Exports to Western Europe	*Belgian, German, and French Exports to the United States*	*United States Net Exports (— = Imports)*
1950	554	803	−249
1951	420	1,690	−1,270
1952	1,063	898	165
1953	504	1,027	−523
1954	541	538	3
1955	1,460	476	984
1956	813	940	−127
1957	822	684	138
1958	402	941	−539
1959	215	2,346	−2,131

Source: aggregated from United Nations, Economic Commission for Europe, *Statistics of World Trade in Steel, 1913–1959* (Geneva, 1961).

There is likely to be communication of expectations between countries, but not an identity of views. In 1936–37, when the United States first thought that prices would rise and then changed its mind, the rest of the world lagged behind in its opinion, with the result that the United States had an import surplus during the twelve months through August 1937 and a big export surplus during the similar period immediately following. The raw materials boom starting in June 1950 did not engage all countries equally. Germany and the United States had elastic expectations, and stocked up hurriedly, through March 1951. Great Britain, on the other hand, stayed out of the market for primary products and used up its stocks. In consequence, it was obliged to replenish inventories at the high average prices prevailing after March 1951, with adverse effects on its reserve position. Figure 13–1 illustrates how for Great Britain and the Netherlands stocks of raw materials and international reserves are alternatives. This illustrates directly the destabilizing effects of inventories on the balance of trade, though only very indirectly the stabilizing consequences for prices and income.

FIGURE 13–1. Balance of Trade and Change in the Physical Volume of Stocks, Netherlands and United Kingdom, 1947–1957

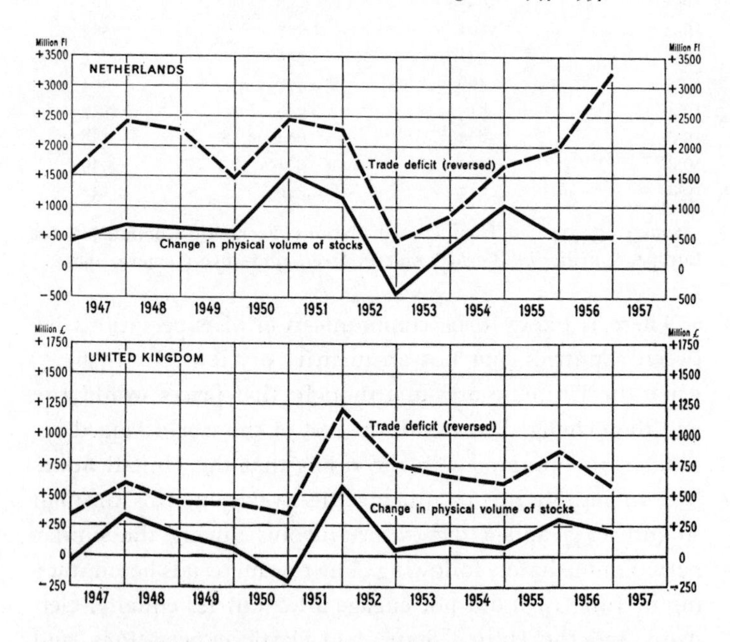

Source: Bank for International Settlements, *Twenty-seventh Annual Report, 1st April 1956–31st March 1957* (Basle, June 3, 1957), p. 55.

Effects of Trade on Stability

The stabilizing effects of foreign trade on national income as a whole take us into the realm of balance-of-payments adjustment theory, which lies outside our province. This much may be said, however: the subject is complex. Whereas imports may generally be said to be an alternative to domestic expenditure (and exports an addition to it), so that a rise in domestic expenditure will be dampened through a spillover into imports, other connections are possible. As noted in an earlier chapter, an increase in domestic output and expenditure may make it possible to cut down on imports, because new production consists of goods previously bought abroad. Or imports may be complementary to domestic investment, so that the availability of, say, capital equipment from abroad stimulates investment at home and leads to income expansion. This was a particular problem at the time of the Marshall Plan: when foreign aid consisted of consumers' goods, and when the local-currency proceeds resulting from their sale in the domestic market was frozen, foreign aid stabilized the domestic economy, absorbing income and mopping up money. When the foreign aid took the form of capital equipment, however, and especially when counterpart funds were used for investment, foreign aid could be said to be destabilizing. Something of the same range of possibilities exists on the export side, but the general rule here is that changes in exports lead to changes in domestic income.

Another exception must be made for foreign capital movements. In ignoring them thus far, we have tacitly assumed that capital has moved only in response to changes in the current account—i.e., like gold, to balance the accounts. But these capital movements can be autonomous, as well as induced, with respect to the balance of payments, and can be either stabilizing or destabilizing to the economy.

In the period from 1870 to 1914 British foreign investment moved opposite total new construction representing domestic capital formation. But in the period of the 1920s and 1930s United States foreign investment was pro- rather than anticyclical. When business was booming and raw materials prices were high, both domestic and foreign investment flourished; when depression came, the credit standing of the borrowing countries fell, and with it the long-term capital outflow.

STABILITY IN PRIMARY PRODUCERS

In the previous chapter it was indicated that foreign trade helps to "balance" the economies of underdeveloped countries by providing outlets for goods produced in surplus and sources of equipment and materials needed. There may be times when foreign sources of supply let a developing country down. India complained after 1950 that it was unable to obtain foreign steel for its development program at any price. The contribution of trade to growth, however, is broadly evident. What about stability?

The stability question in underdeveloped countries has two facets: one cyclical, one secular—the former connected with the role of exports in the cycles of primary-producing countries, the latter with the risks of specialization in products subject to technical change.

More generally, however, underdeveloped countries are unable to enjoy much stability because of their lack of control over the factors determining their income. H. C. Wallich has ventured the generalization that the ratios of exports, investment, and government expenditures to national income are characteristically different in underdeveloped and developed countries.[1] The importance of the relative ratios, of course, is that since domestic investment and government expenditure are subject to national control, while exports are not, a high ratio of exports to national income means that the country has little control over the course of its income. The level of exports depends on incomes abroad and inventory policy, and only to a limited extent on what takes place at home. Wallich believes that in underdeveloped countries the ratio of exports to national income (X/Y) tends to be higher than either the ratio of investment to income (I/Y) or the ratio of government expenditure to income (G/Y). Table 13–2 shows that there is something but not a great deal to this. This table groups countries by categories based on the relation of exports to other components in national income. It turns out that there are developed and underdeveloped countries in each of the four categories.

If the quantitative differences are not striking, there may yet be qualitative ones, suggested by Wallich. The primary-product exporter, or the export economy, has a poorly developed capital market and a relatively underdeveloped domestic sector. When exports rise, two consequences follow. The profitability of exports makes further investment in the sector profitable, so that investment rises. And the underdeveloped state of the capital market means that government is not well placed to borrow for expenditure, with the consequence that government expenditure waits on revenue. As exports rise, taxes rise. This would normally have a stabilizing effect, but the government has many projects waiting, and responds to added tax receipts by enlarging expendi-

1. "Underdeveloped Countries and the International Monetary Mechanism," in *Money, Trade, and Economic Growth* (New York, Macmillan, 1951), pp. 15–32.

TABLE 13–2. *Relative Sizes of Exports (X), Investment (I), and Government Spending (G), as a Proportion of Income (Y), 1958*

Country	X/Y *(1958)*
$X > I + G$	
Luxembourg	103
Trinidad-Tobago	94
Puerto Rico	58
Netherlands	57
British Guiana (1957)	55
Belgian Congo	52
Cyprus	51
Denmark	41
Cuba (1957)	40
Panama	38
Ceylon	36
Eire	33
Ghana	32
Tanganyika	29
Morocco	27
Belgium	23
$X > I$ *and* $X > G$	
Norway	52
Rhodesia and Nyasaland	47
Venezuela	41
Union of South Africa	38
Jamaica (1957)	34
Switzerland	34
Austria	32
Costa Rica	32
Germany	31
New Zealand	30
Sweden	30
Ecuador	24
$X > I$ *and* $X > G$ *(continued)*	
Great Britain	24
Honduras (1957)	24
Guatemala	22
Portugal	20
Egypt (1956)	19
Nigeria (1957)	18
Mexico	17
Chile	14
Philippines	14
$X > I$ *or* $X > G$	
Iceland	37
Peru (1957)	31
Finland	30
Canada	25
Burma	23
China (Taiwan)	23
Australia	19
Italy	18
Japan	16
Brazil	9
$X < I$ *and* $X < G$	
France	17
Israel	14
Greece	13
India (1956)	7
United States	6
Spain (1957)	6

Note: Investment does not include inventory accumulation.
Source: United Nations, *Yearbook of National Accounts Statistics, 1959.*

ture. In consequence, *I* and *G* depend on *X* in an export economy, in contrast to the development economy where they may be larger and are independent. There is some offset to this instability, however, in the fact that these countries tend to have a high propensity to import, and therefore a low multiplier, which contributes stability.

These differences mean that whereas foreign trade tends to stabilize economic activity in developed countries, it destabilizes export economies. This can be related back to what was said at the outset of the chapter. Foreign trade dampens internally stimulated fluctuations and communicates to the interior those which originate abroad. If investment and government expenditure are relatively large and independent variables in developed economies, changes in spending and income have a greater chance of originating at home. In the export economy, as a rule, government spending and private investment were typically linked closely to exports, so that major fluctuations in expenditure were likely to originate abroad. But this was before the adoption of development programs.

MONETARY PROBLEMS OF AN EXPORT ECONOMY[2]

It follows from this that the international monetary mechanism is stabilizing for developed countries which initiate disturbances—apart perhaps from cases of destabilizing short-term capital movements—and destabilizing for underdeveloped. In the expansive phase of the business cycle, outward gold flows, tightened interest rates, and monetary policy restrain expansion in the developed country. But the oppo-

2. This is the title of a book by H. C. Wallich on the money mechanism in Cuba (Cambridge, Mass., 1950).

site occurs in the export economy. The rise of exports in response to increased demands abroad loosens rather than tightens the monetary system as gold or foreign exchange is accumulated. If foreign lending is positively correlated with the cycle in response to investment needs for primary products in the developing countries, there may be an additional source of instability. With rising exports comes rising investment financed by foreign capital. On this showing, the international monetary mechanism is alleged to be stabilizing for developed countries and destabilizing for the primary producers.

There are means of offsetting this disability of the export economy, but they require a degree of self-control that seems to be beyond the capacity of human nature. In the rising phase of the cycle, the primary-producing country should deliberately pursue an anticyclical policy, possibly taxing the proceeds of incremental exports, and freezing them in foreign exchange, or deliberately cutting government expenditure and using the surplus of receipts over expenditures to buy up and sterilize foreign exchange. These techniques depart from the rules of the traditional gold standard, which imply that when a country accumulates gold or foreign exchange it should expand. But it must be remembered that the traditional gold standard first evolved in Britain, a leading industrial country, and is not necessarily applicable without modification to the rest of the world.

One modification of the gold standard used to be applied widely in colonial areas—the requirement of 100 per cent reserves in foreign exchange for domestic currency which formed a large proportion of the total money supply, in contrast to the fractional reserve ratios of final money to international reserves in developed countries. Thus the currency in circulation in Malaya, the British West African colonies, and even in Cuba, used to be based, one-for-one, on reserves of sterling (or dollars). In some cases, such as Cuba, the dollar circulated at par along with the domestic currency. With this limited ratio, expansion based on rising exports could not go far, and contraction found foreign exchange available to pay for import surpluses. With greater independence of policy in these areas, however, has come insistence on fractional reserve expansion ratios, and central bank lending to government, of the same sort as in developed economies. If the one-for-one currency ratio is abandoned, other techniques must be devised to preserve stability. The same rules cannot be applied regardless of whether the disturbances originate at home or abroad.

Primary-producing countries would prefer, of course, measures of commodity price stabilization undertaken by the industrial countries. Their arguments are these: (1) part of the instability is due to destabilizing speculation on the demand side, as well as the short-run inelasticity of supply or (sometimes and) long-run excessive supply responses; (2) if the exporting country undertakes to even out prices, it stabilizes incomes, but destabilizes its balance of payments, whereas if the importing country accumulates and reduces stocks, exports will be maintained in depression and dampened in prosperity so that both incomes and foreign trade are smoothed; and (3) the ability to pay must be taken into account—the industrial countries on the whole are better able to afford to lock up capital in this way. What inhibits international commodity price stabilization, however, is not unwillingness but inability to work out schemes that do not set too high a price, encourage overproduction, and finally break down, with the resulting necessity of dumping accumulated stocks on the market or in the ocean.

RISKS OF SPECIALIZATION

Chapter 6 dealt with technological change. Underdeveloped countries are keenly aware of the risks of specialization in international trade, and of the elimination or reduction in the demand for guano, raw silk, natural rubber, indigo, quinine, chicle, vegetable oils—not to mention the threats to wool, jute, sisal, and coffee. A hydrogenation process for making protein out of wood worried ranchers, who saw oaken steaks as a substitute for beef; and the synthesis of chlorophyll may pose an even wider threat. There can be little doubt that we live in a world of change. But this is hardly an argument not to live.

The risks of specialization attack all sectors of the economy, not just those working for foreign trade; and advanced countries are as vulnerable as the underdeveloped. The essence of economic growth, in Schumpeter's phrase, is creative destruction. The factory replaces home industry, the assembly line replaces the factory bench. Fifteen thousand men were thrown out of work in the North American Aviation plant at Los Angeles when the contract for the Navajo missile was canceled because its specifications failed to meet standards. Companies that have grown rich on the manufacture of propellers have to find other tasks in the jet age; and a fortune made in any business is best preserved by choosing the judicious moment to reinvest in a different field.

It is argued that dependence on exports of resource products means that resources become too specialized to permit a country to turn to alternative employment when demand falls. This may be so; but the answer is not to turn immediately from foreign trade in resource products but to supplement them with the education and training that will make it possible to convert when the moment for doing so arrives. If specialization leads to fossilization, an external diseconomy is involved. The business is worth pursuing only if it can bear a tax that will pay for the training necessary to prevent complete specialization. But this modification would still leave most countries highly specialized in foreign trade.

Economic policy continuously faces the dilemma of whether to adapt to the dictates of the market, or of efficiency, and thereby to cause harm to some social unit that deserves well of society; or whether to temper the wind to the shorn lamb and forestall economic adaptation, preserving the social objective but undermining economic efficiency.

The classic example is the contrast between the British and French responses to the fall in the price of wheat after 1875. In Britain the price collapse was allowed to dismantle agriculture as it had operated—to remove a quarter of a million agricultural workers from the farms, driving them into urban slums, and to depopulate the countryside.[3] In France, on the other hand, the family farm was preserved by raising the tariff on wheat, in 1881, 1892, and again in 1910, with the result that French agriculture, cushioned by high prices, stayed inefficient, highly labor-intensive, and without capital.[4] The step was taken in the name of social stability.[5] It would appear that a country is damned if it does and damned if it doesn't. But this appearance is misleading.

3. Polanyi, *The Great Transformation.*

4. Michel Augé-Laribé, *La Politique agricole de la France de 1880 à 1950* (Paris, Presses Universitaires de France, 1950). The dean of French agricultural experts until his death, M. Augé-Laribé delivers a scathing denunciation of Méline, the author of the tariff of 1892, attacking the tariff as an evasion of the basic necessity for agricultural adaptation.

5. Henri Sée, *Histoire économique de la France,* 2 (Paris, Colin, 1939), 308, 366. Sée thoroughly approves of the "grand harmony" between agriculture and industry.

What is called for by technological change, discovery, or alteration in demand is adaptation. Britain lost a chance to readapt its agriculture even more strongly in favor of the protective foods—eggs, milk, butter, cheese, poultry—by moving more slowly to adapt than neighboring Denmark and the Netherlands, and far-away New Zealand, which benefited from its free-trade policy. It may have been wise for France to impose a tariff on imports for a brief period, to help while more basic adaptive measures were being taken. Augé-Laribé writes: "Everybody said better methods: fertilizer, seed selection, irrigation, roads, drainage, cheaper transport and education. Immediately. But they did not do it even slowly."[6] To evade specialization in exports or to cut off imports may be a reasonable step to protect social values during a period of adjustment—all parts of society should be shielded from sharp blows when they cannot protect themselves. But the adaptation should take place. Resisting the changes called for by the market is likely to produce worse results in the long run than any possible short-term harm which the transitional process may inflict.

6. Augé-Laribé, p. 80.

14 THE EFFECTS OF TRADE ON SOCIAL AND POLITICAL LIFE

THE FAMILY AS A PRODUCING UNIT

In traditional societies the family is not only a social but also an economic unit, engaged in production as well as consumption. Agricultural experts point out that the distinctive characteristic of the peasant is that his family and the productive unit are coextensive. And almost the same thing can be said for the artisan, the household handicraft worker, and the small retail entrepreneur.

Foreign trade, like any extension of the market economy, may be a threat to the family as a productive unit. Typically unable to produce for export, because of incapacity to produce a standardized product in quantity and to achieve the requisite marketing, the family is frequently threatened by imports that can be produced more efficiently and on a larger scale elsewhere in the world where the land is more fertile, or where more land-intensive or capital-intensive methods are put to profitable use.

Exceptions do exist—in the cocoa producers of West Africa for instance, and in the peasant rubber production of Malaya; also we must include the Danish family farm, which produces dairy products and bacon, and markets them through cooperatives. Farming is a family matter too in Areas of Recent Settlement, although in the United States it is beginning to be the commercial, corporative agriculture that produces the export surpluses, while the average family farm is unable to export without subsidy. But in the rest of the world the family farm typically produces only limited surpluses. Exports are the product of specialized units. In a few very labor-intensive lines, like fruit, vegetables, and wines, the units may be of family size. They are more likely to be plantations, *latifundias, haciendas, fincas.* These are labor- or land-intensive, and sometimes produce what are called "hunger exports," that is, surpluses of grain harvested by labor that is poorly paid and fed, despite living on the land. The general experience of land reform in Eastern Europe is that agricultural exports decline. The worker who receives an allotment from a landed estate sets out as rapidly as he can to buy a cow and raise chickens and pigs. The surplus of grain vanishes, exports decline. The peasant and the land work harder; the farmer and his family eat better.

Another illustration of the inability of family industry to export is furnished by India, where there are two sections of the cotton textile industry—one, cottage industry, using hand equipment; the other, factories, using machines. To prevent unemployment in the cottage-industry sector, taxes and quantity limitations are imposed on factory output, but these are remitted to the extent that the factories sell in export markets, as the cottage industry cannot.

The difficulties experienced by the family unit in withstanding competition of imports hardly need demonstration. The European peasant provides the prime example in the twentieth century—in Germany, Switzerland, Italy, and France—as the handloom weavers and charcoal forges did in the nineteenth. The Scottish producers of Harris tweed are a distinguished exception. As a rule, however, the artisan can survive only in localized service industries—tailoring, shoemaking, plumbing, and the restaurant trade. Economies of scale in the production of movable products have spelled his doom for all except the most highly skilled crafts, like goldleaf manufacturing or diamond cutting; or the lowest paid, like Philippine embroidering.

The need for a special regime for agriculture in international trade is basically related to this incompatibility between family enterprise and efficient scale. Legislation in favor of fair-trade practices—and retail price maintenance—and against the spread of chain stores has the same roots in the attempt to protect the family enterprise from the encroachment of more efficient larger units, but these fields of endeavor lie outside international trade.

Capacity to export or to meet the competition of imports almost always then implies a scale of production larger than the typical family-size unit.[1] Where the family is an important source of social cohesion, there is likely to be some ambiguity about foreign trade. Everyone, or practically everyone, welcomes the higher income associated with more effi-

1. A distinction should be made between the family enterprise at the level of the artisan or cottage industry, and the "family firm," which David S. Landes, for example, thinks characterized the French economy: "French Entrepreneurship and Industrial Growth in the Nineteenth Century," *Journal of Economic History, 9* (1949), 45–61. Their attitudes are in some ways similar but the competence of the family firm, and its capacity to participate in trade, were far higher.

cient production, but many people in such societies regret the hurt to the family unit. This is likely to color attitudes toward foreign trade. Perhaps France furnishes the best example. Its producers were said not to be "export-minded,"[2] to be "poor at trade, with a take it or leave it attitude,"[3] to have "an ancient tradition of neglecting exports,"[4] to have the "instinct for exports poorly developed,"[5] or, if they ever had it, "to have lost the habit of exporting."[6] With respect to imports, moreover, French economic literature argues heatedly whether agriculture or industry received the greater protection. Most observers agree that there has been protection for everybody,[7] and that France turned inward—prior to World War II, at least—and more and more isolated itself from world markets.[8]

France can be contrasted in these aspects with Britain, where family unity and continuity are very much less, and with Germany. German feeling against agricultural imports was fully as strong as French, but, in the field of industry, armaments and exports were both regarded as contributing to the strength of the state, hence honorific.[9]

2. Henry W. Ehrmann, *Organized Business in France* (Princeton, Princeton University Press, 1957), p. 395, n. 58.

3. Dunham, *Industrial Revolution in France*, p. 382.

4. George Passe, *Economies comparées de la France et de la Grande-Bretagne* (Paris, Fayard, 1957), p. 196.

5. Ehrmann, p. 394.

6. Warren C. Baum, *The French Economy and the State* (Princeton, Princeton University Press, 1958), p. 341.

7. Charles Bettelheim, *Bilan de l'économie française, 1919–1946* (Paris, Presses Universitaires de France, 1947), pp. 172 ff. Augé-Laribé, *La Politique agricole,* had insisted that the peasant sold in relatively unprotected markets, bought in protected. Others have seen the cause of French stagnation in agricultural protection. The answer seems clear that the French system provided protection for everybody.

8. Augé-Laribé, p. 56.

9. Parker, "Entrepreneurial Opportunities," p. 32.

What replaced family enterprise as a result of economic units of sufficient size to export and to meet the competition of imports? Mainly the urban factory, a subject which goes well beyond foreign trade and is too vast for discussion here. Particularly relevant to our subject, however, is efficiently organized primary production—the plantation, ranch, mine, and lumber camp, which are regarded in some quarters as inacceptable social substitutes for the family enterprise. We have touched on the criticism that the plantation involves a once-and-for-all change in technique, thereafter fossilized.[10] It is also objected that the work of plantations with a large seasonal fluctuation is socially demoralizing; idleness during the dead season produces uprootedness and delinquency.[11] Similarly there is concern in Canada over heavy emphasis on mining and timber, which are thought to be not highly cultural activities, however lucrative.[12]

There is in all this, as in a great deal of the economic reasoning of the layman (including, along with the man in the street, the writer of newspaper editorials and the political orator), a strong admixture of the *post hoc, ergo propter hoc* fallacy. This fallacy is met most frequently in economics in the assertion that since rich countries have industry, the way to get rich is to industrialize. High levels of culture are in fact the product of cities, with which commerce, administration, and industry are associated, but the first task may be to specialize and increase productivity, rather than to

10. See above, p. 102.

11. F. Ortiz, *Cuban Counterpoint* (New York, Knopf, 1947). This Cuban sociologist stressed the contrasts between sugar, with its deadening impacts, and tobacco, with its demands for skill, year-round employment, and so on. Since the book was written, however, the cigar-making machine has altered the picture.

12. Royal Commission on Canada's Economic Prospects (W. L. Gordon, chairman), *Final Report.*

move directly from primary to secondary and tertiary, without any assurance that these activities can be performed effectively.

Trade also has an impact on the traditional way of life in consumption. The demonstration effect produces an increase in consumer choice that is usually welcomed, but not when it alters traditional ways of doing things and displaces them with foreign ways. This can be seen in the disfavor with which Coca-Cola, blue jeans, and jazz have been held in certain parts of Europe. Another manifestation which rings a familiar note is the outcry in a Thailand newspaper against eggs and bacon for breakfast, and an appeal to uphold the traditional succulent and nutritious breakfast of fish soup.[13] It has been observed that the shift from subsistence to plantation life and purchased goods, frequently imported grain, has reduced the dietary balance of traditional societies. So widespread and homogeneous are consumption standards becoming that it is comforting to recall some institutions, like the European continental breakfast, which resist corruption. On the whole, however, it is impossible to argue that the negative effects of trade on consumption are more than a minuscule offset to the positive effects on both consumption and production.

REGIONAL IMPACTS

Trade alters the income distribution not only of factors of production as a whole in a country but also of different regions. When factor markets are less than perfect, there may be differences in factor combinations between a capital-intensive industry in the North of the United States, for example, and a labor- and land-intensive cotton culture in

13. *New York Times* (July 4, 1955), p. 7.

the South. The interests of the two sections will differ in trade policy, as we are very much aware in United States economic history. The same can be said for eastern and western Germany (before World War II), the rest of Canada against Ontario and Quebec, southern and northern Italy, labor-intensive sugar and land-intensive meat in Argentina, land-intensive coffee and labor-intensive urban industry in Brazil, and so on. These distributional effects may influence not only trade policy—whether to move toward freer trade or greater protection—but also more subtle questions of the exchange rate. An overvalued rate will lower the costs of imported foodstuffs and consumers' goods. Combined with import restrictions on the industrial output of nonwage goods to balance the accounts, it strongly favors urban industry, while hurting export interests. The latter, on the other hand, benefit from devaluation and removal of import controls. The political interplay between these forces, plus inflation, have produced one hundred years of exchange depreciation in Brazil.

In nineteenth-century Britain, Manchester was the seat of free-trade agitation, led by Richard Cobden and John Bright, while the landed interests favored retention of the Corn Laws. But Birmingham was lukewarm to free trade, and in fact produced Joseph Chamberlain, the first spokesman in the 1890s for Empire preference. Empire preference may be regarded as a simple variant of tariffs to help exporters in industries lagging behind world competition, and this should presumably have appealed to Manchester cotton textile exporters, as well as to Birmingham industrialists. But tradition counts in these questions: Manchester had a long tradition of free trade, and Birmingham did not. Birmingham had historically been a city of many small industries, based originally on wrought iron and later, when reserves of coal and iron ore had been exhausted, on imported steel. Early exports of hardware, jewelry, buttons, and metalware met early competition in domestic markets in Europe and the United States, and when it turned to more complex products in the engineering field, Birmingham was only partly an exporter and competed with imports from Europe and the United States over a considerable range of products. Gradually Birmingham in the Midlands wrested leadership in commercial policy from Manchester in the North, and assisted in bringing about the change in British trade policy.[14]

Regional interests change. In the United States it used to be that the South was for free trade, the North, and particularly the Northeast, against. With the rise of mass production Detroit came to be the spokesman for reciprocal reductions of trade barriers, at first hesitantly and falteringly, but later with confidence. With today's imports of small cars, Detroit may no longer be sure. Texas equally has altered its principles, as oil exports have given way to imports; and the Carolinas and Georgia have changed their perspective, as production of cotton for export has moved to Texas, Arizona, New Mexico, and California, and the newly established Southern textile industry labors under import competition. Finally, New England, the home of protection, where the textile industry started, is revising its views in the opposite sense: a consumer of residual fuel and heating oils, it sees little gain from restrictions on oil imports; and as textile and shoe production, not to mention fishing, have given way to electronics and the tourist trade, the fervor for protectionism as a principle is inevitably diluted.

14. W. H. B. Court, *A Concise Economic History of Britain from 1750 to Recent Times* (Cambridge, Cambridge University Press, 1954), pp. 217–18.

TRADE AND THE SIZE OF THE SOVEREIGN UNIT

Foreign trade can thus be divisive of national unity and a subject of contention among constituent elements of the domestic polity. But there is another aspect of foreign trade that has come into more and more prominence since World War II. This is economic integration between or among countries, at least in its partial aspects of a customs union, and occasionally in relation to the deeper political process of federation or merging of sovereignties.

In the nineteenth century the world had only one significant example of customs union—Zollverein, and this led to, or at least was followed by, political unification. Unification occurred under the strong leadership of Prussia and in the wake of a succession of wars. The example raises sharply, however, the question of the connection between close economic cooperation and international political relations.

We need not discuss the differences among a "free-trade area," in which each country retains its own tariff against the outside world, but no tariff vis-à-vis the other members; "customs union," where a common tariff is agreed; and "economic union," which goes further in harmonizing tax and other policies. Nor is it necessary to remind the reader that steps toward economic integration in trade are required, if they are, only because universal free trade is unattainable. Lowering one set of trade barriers in a world where others remain may or may not improve the allocation of world resources, as Jacob Viner has pointed out.[15] In addition to widening consumer choice, customs union (to use the term as a generic one) may stimulate production in low-cost

15. *The Customs Union Issue* (New York, 1950). See also the discussion of second-best policies, above, pp. 147 ff.

sources in the area and cut back high-cost inefficient output. But it may also expand inefficient sources of production in the area at the expense of low-cost producers in third countries. Thus trade may be created inside the union, or diverted from pre-existing trade with the outside world, even assuming that the tariff of the customs union is not higher than the "average tariff" of the constituent countries, however computed. If the new tariff is higher than the average, trade diversion is more certain. Where the extension of the market permits advantage to be taken of economies of scale, on the other hand, the likelihood is that customs union will be trade-creating.

Our question, however, does not concern the economics of integration, which goes well beyond the scope of this study,[16] but rather the effects of trade on political life. It goes without saying that political integration leads to economic integration, or at least to customs union among the constituents of the larger political unit.[17] The issue is whether economic

16. For a thorough discussion see Bela Balassa, *The Theory of Economic Integration* (Homewood, Ill., Irwin, 1961).

17. Whether customs union and economic integration are identical depends upon one's definition of the latter. There must surely be free trade, and a considerable amount of it. A customs union between Iceland and New Zealand would hardly lead to economic integration in a meaningful sense, since transport barriers are so great, and mutual trade so limited, that the latter's effects would be negligible. Some economists —Gunnar Myrdal in *The International Economy* is one—define "economic integration" as that amount of trade and factor movements that bring about factor price equalization. On this definition, it is evident that economic integration has been missing within many countries, where dual economies exist, or where different factor proportions persist in different regions—for example, the North and South of the United States before World War II, and to a lesser degree thereafter. Others, such as Jan Tinbergen in *International Economic Integration* (Amsterdam, Elsevier, 1953), identify economic integration with free trade.

integration, or customs union, constitutes a step toward political unification.

As in so much of history, the problem is to disentangle causes from symptoms. The Zollverein was but one step on the road to German unification, which had far deeper roots in a common language and heritage, including, particularly, defeat at the hands of Napoleon. Complete unification waited primarily on the development of transport and communication networks to crystallize the unifying social, political, and cultural forces. As one step leads to another, without causing it, so the Zollverein doubtless assisted the process of unification by demonstrating the possibility of working together, creating patterns of communication, and breaking down political and social barriers where they remained.

Rather than economic integration leading to political and social integration, it seems that a high degree of the latter is required before the former can be achieved. The successful Belgian-Luxembourg Economic Union does not illustrate this well, since this is domination rather than a partnership. Luxembourg is so small, and its independence so nominal, that it can safely be added to Belgian interests without in any way diluting them. But the Belgian economic union with the Netherlands has been something else again. This has been in the process of creation since 1944, when agreement was reached between exiled governments in London to combine the two economies after the war. The path has been a long one. For a time, progress was inhibited by Dutch balance-of-payments difficulties, due to war destruction, which threatened the monetary stability of the partnership. Later there were problems of freeing capital movements at a time when rather different monetary policies were being pursued in the two countries. But the greatest difficulty has been faced in that sector which so frequently demands special treatment because of its social organization—agriculture. Industrial tariffs could be removed without too great difficulty, as could restrictions on the movement of capital and labor. Dutch efficiency in growing vegetables, however, and relative Belgian inefficiency presented problems which have still not been completely resolved. For when the Belgian politician was asked to lower the remaining barriers to free entry of Dutch vegetables, the question was squarely posed whether the Belgian farmer should be liquidated because he was inefficient, or preserved because he was, after all, Belgian. In the end, the signing of the Rome treaty and the vague promise of a special regime for agriculture in the European Economic Community made it possible to back away from this crucial test. It remains to be faced in the Common Market. In June 1961 France, whose farmers have become relatively efficient, was exerting pressure on Germany, whose farmers are highly protected, for faster progress on the special regime for agriculture, by delaying the earlier-agreed acceleration of the stages by which the treaty takes effect.

The same critical test is being faced or deferred in other countries. In Central and Latin America, Africa, and the Middle East many countries hopefully eye customs union as an outlet for nascent manufacturing industries, without paying as yet much attention to the necessity of admitting competition for some and death to others. When this necessity is faced, customs unions often break down for lack of the essential political solidarity. Just as Colombia and Bolivia have held aloof from the Montevideo treaty, despite its escape clauses, because of worry that they will not be able to accept its commitments to duty-free imports, and Turkey and Greece express their political support for the Six but explain that they are unable to join it for imports (much as they would like to for exports), so others, when the time comes, may find it difficult to carry economic commitments through.

The future of the European Economic Community is far brighter. There is inability to agree in detail about agriculture. There is a fundamental political difference in attitude between General de Gaulle, who sees the Community as a vehicle for French leadership and *grandeur,* and Chancellor Adenauer, who emphasizes the submergence of national characteristics into European oneness. But on all sides in industry is the strong insistence on efficiency for survival, and the readiness—for the first time in many industries in France—to let the inefficient firm go under.

There is also little doubt that the process of competing in industry and collaborating in government, provided it comes out this way and not the reverse, will strengthen the tendencies already at work to merge national sovereignties. The process may well stop short of federation. This is particularly likely if the British succeed in negotiating an economic accommodation, for they are likely to balk at completely submerging their sovereignty in a European, as opposed to a Commonwealth or North Atlantic federation. But growing trade (rapidly growing, as pointed out in Chapter 2) may interlace Western Europe with communication that will cultivate the existing sense of cohesion and identity to the point where political integration will follow.

TRADE AND PEACE

It is a well-known text of orators that foreign trade fosters peace. The phrase is "peace and prosperity." There is little doubt, if political units are prepared to put through the required adjustments, that trade can contribute significantly to prosperity. It probably has little effect on the incidence of war.

Civil wars are a case in point: they occur between regional or social segments closely linked in trade. The violent separation of Pakistan from India occurred despite intimate trade connections that made the two portions of British India interdependent. Since partition, India has duplicated the jute and cotton production for which it had previously depended on Pakistan, and East Pakistan has duplicated a portion of Indian capacity in the manufacture of burlap.

Nor can we accept the opposite theory that competition for trade leads to war. A high degree of specialization leads to dependence on overseas sources of supply, and threats to these "vital interests"—Middle East oil, Southeast Asian rubber and tin—may in some sense enhance the alacrity with which force is used. But there is little support for the Marxist belief in the necessity of imperial war for markets to absorb surplus production. Trade had little or nothing to do with even the acquisition of African colonies after 1875, which drew its stimulus largely from interests of "national prestige."[18] A case can be made that economic interests played a role in the Mexican War of 1846, the Spanish-American War of 1898, and the attack on Mexico in 1916. But by and large, trade has little explanatory value as a cause of the two world wars, the War of 1870, the Korean Conflict, and any number more that could be named.

There is probably something to be said on the positive side. Trade flourishes in peacetime—witness Franco-German trade in coal and steel under the Schuman Plan, or United States-Canadian trade along that unfortified border—and trade creates communication channels that may serve further to promote understanding. One cannot afford to be categorical on the point. In some cases to know is to find differences,

18. Henri Brunschwig, *Mythes et réalités de l'impérialisme colonial français, 1871–1914* (Paris, Colin, 1960).

rather than similarities, and to promote dislike rather than understanding. But in general, and despite the fact that the connection is indirect, perhaps remote, trade can probably be counted on the positive side as a contributor to peace. The justification of foreign trade, however, lies less in international politics than in its contribution to the economic well-being of the trading world.

BIBLIOGRAPHY

BIBLIOGRAPHIES

Allen, Robert L., "Soviet Bloc Foreign Economic Relations: An English Language Bibliography," Department of State, Bureau of Intelligence and Research, External Research Paper 134, June 1958.

American Economic Association, *Readings in the Theory of International Trade,* Homewood, Ill., Irwin (formerly Philadelphia, Blakiston Co.), 1949. (Bibliography of articles.)

Hazlewood, Arthur, *The Economics of "Under-Developed" Areas,* 2d enlarged ed. London, Oxford University Press, 1959.

Johns Hopkins University, Department of Political Economy, *Economic Library Selections,* ser. 2, no. 1, *International Economics,* December 1954.

GENERAL TREATISES

Classic (in chronological order)

Smith, Adam, *An Inquiry into the Nature and Causes of the Wealth of Nations,* 1776.

Ricardo, David, *On the Principles of Political Economy and Taxation,* 1817.

Mill, John Stuart, *Principles of Political Economy,* 1848.

Cairnes, J. E., *Some Leading Principles of Political Economy Newly Expounded,* New York, Harper, 1874.

Bastable, Charles F., *The Theory of International Trade,* 4th ed. London, Macmillan, 1903.

Marshall, Alfred, *Money, Credit and Commerce,* London, Macmillan, 1923.

Edgeworth, F. Y., *Papers Relating to Political Economy, 3,* London, Macmillan, 1925.

Taussig, Frank W., *International Trade,* New York, Macmillan, 1927.

Modern Formulations

American Economic Association, *Readings in the Theory of International Trade,* Homewood, Ill., Irwin, 1949.

Caves, Richard E., *Trade and Economic Structure: Models and Methods,* Cambridge, Mass., Harvard University Press, 1960.

Haberler, Gottfried, *The Theory of International Trade, with Its Applications to Commercial Policy,* trans. A. Stonier and F. Benham, New York, Macmillan, 1936, 2d ed. 1950.

Meade, James E., *The Theory of International Economic Policy:* vol. 2, *Trade and Welfare,* London and New York, Oxford University Press, 1955.

Ohlin, Bertil, *Interregional and International Trade,* Cambridge, Mass., Harvard University Press, 1933.

Viner, Jacob, *Studies in the Theory of International Trade,* New York, Harper, 1937.

Textbooks

Byé, Maurice, *Relations économiques internationales,* Paris, Dalloz, 1959.

Ellsworth, Paul T., *The International Economy,* rev. ed. New York, Macmillan, 1958.

Harrod, Sir Roy, *International Economics,* rev. ed. London, J. Nisbet, 1957.

Kindleberger, Charles P., *International Economics,* rev. ed. Homewood, Ill., Irwin, 1958.

FACTUAL TREATISES AND DISCUSSIONS

Allen, R. G. D., and Ely, J. E., eds., *International Trade Statistics,* New York, Wiley, 1953.

Condliffe, John B., *The Commerce of Nations,* New York, Norton, 1950.

General Agreement on Tariffs and Trade, *International Trade,* Geneva (annual).

Hirschman, Albert O., *National Power and the Structure of Foreign Trade,* Berkeley, University of California Press, 1945.

Lamartine Yates, P., *Forty Years of Foreign Trade,* London, Allen and Unwin, 1959.

League of Nations (F. Hilgerdt), *Europe's Trade,* Geneva, 1941.

———*The Network of World Trade,* Geneva, 1942.

United Nations, *Economic Survey of Europe,* Geneva (annual).

———*World Economic Report,* New York (annual).

Woytinsky, W. S., and Woytinsky, E. S., *World Commerce and Governments,* New York, Twentieth Century Fund, 1955.

THE SKEPTICS

List, Friederich, *Das nationale System der Politischen,* 1887, trans. S. Lloyd, *The National System of Political Economy,* London, Longmans, Green, 1928.

Manoilescu, Mihail, *The Theory of Protection and International Trade,* London, King, 1931.

Myint, Hla, "The Gains from International Trade and the Backward Countries," *Review of Economic Studies, 22* (1954–55), 129–42.

———"An Interpretation of Economic Backwardness," *Oxford Economic Papers,* n.s., *6* (1954), 132–63.

———"The 'Classical Theory' of International Trade and the Underdeveloped Countries," *Economic Journal, 68* (1958), 317–37.

Myrdal, Gunnar, *The International Economy: Problems and Prospects,* New York, Harper, 1956.

Singer, H. W., "The Distribution of Gains between Investing and Borrowing Countries," *American Economic Review, Papers and Proceedings, 40* (1950), 473–85.

United Nations Economic and Social Council, Economic Commission for Latin America (Raul Prebisch), *The Economic Development of Latin America and Its Principal Problems,* Lake Success, United Nations Dept. of Economic Affairs, 1950.

Williams, John H., "The Theory of International Trade Reconsidered," in American Economic Association, *Readings in the Theory of International Trade,* Homewood, Ill., Irwin, 1949.

Bibliography

FUNCTIONAL STUDIES

Trade and Growth

Bhagwati, J., "Immiserizing Growth: A Geometrical Note," *Review of Economic Studies, 25* (1958), 201–05.

Chenery, Hollis B., "Patterns of Industrial Growth," *American Economic Review, 50* (1960), 624–54.

Findlay, R., and Grubert, H., "Factor Intensities, Technological Progress, and the Terms of Trade," *Oxford Economic Papers,* n.s., *11* (1959), 111–21.

Haberler, Gottfried, *International Trade and Economic Development,* Cairo, National Bank of Egypt, 1959.

Hicks, J. R., "An Inaugural Lecture," *Oxford Economic Papers,* n.s., *5* (1953), 117–35.

Johnson, Harry G., *International Trade and Economic Growth,* London, Allen and Unwin, 1958.

League of Nations (F. Hilgerdt), *Industrialization and Foreign Trade,* Geneva, 1945.

Nurkse, Ragnar, *Patterns of Trade and Development,* Stockholm, 1959.

Viner, Jacob, *International Trade and Economic Development,* Glencoe, Ill., Free Press, 1952.

Other

Hexner, Ervin, *International Cartels,* Chapel Hill, University of North Carolina Press, 1945.

Meade, James E., *Problems of Economic Union,* Chicago, University of Chicago Press, 1953.

Stocking, George W., and Watkins, Myron W., *Cartels or Competition?* New York, Twentieth Century Fund, 1948.

United Nations, *Commodity Trade and Economic Development,* New York, 1953.

United Nations Secretariat, Dept. of Economic Affairs, *Instability in Export Markets of Under-Developed Countries,* New York, 1952.

Viner, Jacob, *Dumping: A Problem in International Trade,* Chicago, University of Chicago Press, 1923.

———*The Customs Union Issue,* New York, Carnegie Endowment for International Peace, 1950.
Wu, Yuan-Li, *Economic Warfare,* New York, Prentice-Hall, 1952.

COUNTRY STUDIES[1]

Canada

Brecher, Irving, and Reisman, S. S., *Canada-United States Economic Relations,* Ottawa, Royal Commission on Canada's Economic Prospects, 1957.
Caves, Richard E., and Holton, Richard H., *The Canadian Economy,* Cambridge, Mass., Harvard University Press, 1959.
Innis, Harold R., *Problems of Staple Production in Canada,* Toronto, Ryerson Press, 1933.
Royal Commission on Canada's Economic Prospects (W. L. Gordon, chairman), *Final Report,* Ottawa, H.M.S.O., 1957.
Young, J. H., *Canadian Commercial Policy,* Ottawa, Royal Commission on Canada's Economic Prospects, 1957.

China

Chêng, Yu-k'uei, *Foreign Trade and the Industrial Development of China,* Washington, D.C., University Press of Washington, 1956.
Li, Choh-ming, *Economic Development of Communist China,* Berkeley, University of California Press, 1959.
Remer, C. F., *The Foreign Trade of China,* Shanghai, Commercial Press, 1926.

France

Arnauné, A., *Le Commerce extérieur et les tarifs de douane,* Paris, Alcan, 1911.
Bloch-Lainé, Fr., *La Zone franc,* Paris, Presses Universitaires de France, 1956.
Haight, Frank A., *French Import Quotas,* London, King, 1935.
———*A History of French Commercial Policies,* New York, Macmillan, 1941.

1. Attention is called to the many studies of national economies published by the International Bank for Reconstruction and Development and the Twentieth Century Fund.

Weiller, Jean, and Duvaux, Jacques, *Economie française, échanges extérieurs, et structures internationales,* Cahiers de l'Institut de Science Economique Appliquée, sér. P, no. 1, 1957.

White, Harry D., *The French International Accounts, 1880–1913,* Cambridge, Mass., Harvard University Press, 1933.

Germany

Erhard, Ludwig, *Germany's Comeback in the World Market,* trans. W. H. Johnston, New York, Macmillan, 1954.

Gerschenkron, Alexander, *Bread and Democracy in Germany,* Berkeley, University of California Press, 1943.

Liesner, H. H., *The Import Dependence of Britain and Western Germany: A Comparative Study,* Princeton, International Finance Section, Department of Economics and Sociology, Princeton University, 1957.

India

Lakdawala, D. T., *International Aspects of Indian Economic Development,* London, Oxford University Press, 1951.

Varshney, Roshan Lal, *India's Foreign Trade during and after the Second World War,* Allahabad, Kitab Mahal, 1954.

Japan

Cohen, Jerome B., "Problems in Foreign Trade and Investment," *Annals of the American Academy of Political and Social Science, 308,* 1956.

Lockwood, William W., *The Economic Development of Japan: Growth and Structural Change, 1868–1938,* Princeton, Princeton University Press, 1954.

Latin America

Delwart, Louis O., *The Future of Latin American Exports to the United States: 1965 and 1970,* Washington, D.C., National Planning Association, 1960.

Pan American Union, *International Trade, Industrialization and Economic Growth,* Washington, D.C., 1956.

Wallich, Henry C., *Monetary Problems of an Export Economy,* Cambridge, Mass., Harvard University Press, 1950.

Bibliography

Middle East

Bonné, Alfred, *The Economic Development of the Middle East*, London, Kegan Paul, Trench, Trubner, 1945.
Longrigg, S. H., *Oil in the Middle East*, London, Oxford University Press, 1954, 2d ed. 1961.

Soviet Union and Soviet Bloc

Baykov, Alexander, *Soviet Foreign Trade*, Princeton, Princeton University Press, 1946.
Berliner, Joseph, *Soviet Economic Aid*, New York, Praeger, 1958.
Brzezinski, Zbigniew, *The Soviet Bloc*, Cambridge, Mass., Harvard University Press, 1960.
Cherviakov, P. A., *The Organization and Techniques of Soviet Foreign Trade* (in Russian), Moscow, Vneshtorgizdat, 1958.
Ivanov, N. I., *The Development of the Economic Ties of the European Peoples' Democracies* (in Russian), Moscow, Vneshtorgizdat, 1959.
Nove, Alec, and Donnelly, Desmond, *Trade with Communist Countries*, London, Macmillan, 1960.
Spulber, Nicholas, *The Economics of Communist Eastern Europe*, Cambridge, Mass., Technology Press, 1957.
"State Trading," parts I and II, *Law and Contemporary Problems*, *24*, 1959.

Sweden

Södersten, B., "A Survey of the Structural Development of Sweden's Exports and Imports since 1870," paper submitted to the Sixth European Conference of the International Association for Research in Income and Wealth, Portoroz, 1959.

United Kingdom

Benham, Frederic, *Great Britain under Protection*, New York, Macmillan, 1941.
Imlah, Albert H., *Economic Elements in the Pax Britannica*, Cambridge, Mass., Harvard University Press, 1958.
Kahn, Alfred E., *Great Britain in the World Economy*, New York, Columbia University Press, 1946.

Levi, Leone, *The History of British Commerce and of the Economic Progress of the British Nation,* 2d ed. London, Murray, 1880.

Political and Economic Planning, *Britain and World Trade,* London, 1947.

Robertson, Sir Dennis, *Britain in the World Economy,* London, Allen and Unwin, 1954.

Robinson, E. A. G., "The Changing Structure of the British Economy," *Economic Journal, 64* (1954), 443–61.

Saul, S. B., *Studies in British Overseas Trade, 1870–1914,* Liverpool, Liverpool University Press, 1960.

Schlote, Werner, *Entwicklung und Strukturwandlungen des englischen Ausserhandels von 1700 bis zur Gegenwart,* trans. W. O. Henderson and W. H. Chaloner, *British Overseas Trade from 1700 to the 1930s,* Oxford, Blackwell, 1952.

United States

Aubrey, Henry G., *United States Imports and World Trade,* Oxford, Clarendon Press, 1957.

Hoffmeyer, Erik, *Dollar Shortage and the Structure of U.S. Foreign Trade,* Copenhagen, Munksgaard, 1958.

Humphrey, Don D., *American Imports,* New York, Twentieth Century Fund, 1955.

Kindleberger, Charles P., "International Trade and United States Experience, 1870–1955," in Ralph E. Freeman, ed., *Postwar Economic Trends in the United States,* New York, Harper, 1960.

Lary, Hal B., *The United States in the World Economy,* Washington, D.C., G.P.O., 1943.

Leontief, Wassily, "Domestic Production and Foreign Trade: The American Capital Position Re-examined," *Proceedings* of the American Philosophical Society, 97 (1953), 332–49, reprinted in *Economia Internazionale, 7,* 1954.

MacDougall, Donald, *The World Dollar Problem,* London, Macmillan, 1957.

Piquet, Howard S., *Aid, Trade, and the Tariff,* New York, Crowell, 1953.

Taussig, Frank W., *The Tariff History of the United States,* 8th ed. New York, Putnam's, 1931.

Other

Bauer, P. T., *West African Trade,* Cambridge, Cambridge University Press, 1954.
Ghate, B. G., *Asia's Trade,* New Delhi, Indian Council of World Affairs, 1948.
Meyer, F. V., *Britain's Colonies in World Trade,* Toronto, Oxford University Press, 1948.
Stahl, K. M., *The Metropolitan Organization of British Colonial Trade,* London, Faber and Faber, 1951.

INDEX

Page numbers in italics indicate tabular references

Index

Index

Index

Index

Index

Index

Index

Index